Pennsylvania Beautiful

(EASTERN)

BY
WALLACE NUTTING
Author of the States Beautiful Series, etc.

ILLUSTRATED BY THE AUTHOR WITH MANY
EXAMPLES OF LANDSCAPES AND OLD HOUSES
IN ALL THE COUNTIES HEREIN DESCRIBED

FRAMINGHAM · MASSACHUSETTS
OLD AMERICA CO
PUBLISHERS

THE PLIMPTON PRESS
NORWOOD·MASS·U·S·A

Pennsylvania Beautiful

(EASTERN)

EXPLANATORY

W E DO not promise the reader anything more than about three hundred pictures, mostly selected for their supposed beauty, of eastern Pennsylvania. We do not promise that they shall be evenly distributed over that section of the state. We reserve the right to show more in one section than in another, if time or mood or weather or the greater number of points of interest conduce to this arrangement. Nor do we promise that these pictures shall be arranged in any particular order, such as the reader may expect. We make these disavowals that no one may be disappointed. We believe that we shall be endorsed in saying that many of the pictures are well worth while.

Sometimes it seems to be a disappointment that our books do not provide a picture to a township, or something of that sort. There are many practical reasons why such a method has been found impossible; but a sufficient reason is that the book, if so composed, would not be as interesting.

The author has spent more time in the preparation of this than in any of his previous books of the STATES BEAUTIFUL SERIES. This arises from the fact that while nearly all parts of Pennsylvania are beautiful, except those given over wholly to mining, many of the most beautiful parts are not especially pictorial. The very perfection of cultivation in many of the valleys is such that there is nothing of peculiar interest to record.

The line of demarcation which we have arbitrarily chosen to separate eastern from western Pennsylvania is roughly about on the longitude of Lebanon. There may be an occasional instance in which we go west of that line, and there may be occasional regions east of that line, that are not very fully represented. We have, however, faithfully inspected most of the part of Pennsylvania which we here designate " east." We cover less than half of the state, because it is the older half and the more populous.

Nor is this volume at all history or a story of eastern Pennsylvania. It is a book of pictures primarily and principally. Any observations regarding these pictures are made as there may seem to be a necessity for them, or as the incidents of travel urge them. Let no one look, in the following pages, for all the famous features of eastern Pennsylvania, worthy to be included in the volume. That inclusion would require an encyclopaedia. We are giving as many illustrations as we could, consistently with the design of the series. We have the satisfaction of knowing that we have discovered a great many hitherto unrecorded pictures. The illustrations at least have the merit, with the exception of four or five drawings, which will be credited in their place, of being original. All but a half dozen of the pictures were made in the years 1923 and 1924, and few of them have been seen in any other form than that in which they now appear.

It has been the delight and eager purpose of the writer to get together as many illustrations as possible of that old life in America, which is rapidly passing away. If, however, the reader is a resident in a neighborhood which he does not find represented in these pages, he is quite likely to resent the omission. Many write us expressing surprise at such omissions. What can we do? The inclusion of anything else would simply mean the exclusion of something we show. If, in process of time, this edition is exhausted, any further treatment of this portion of the state will be marked by the inclusion of new neighborhoods. This edition will be the only one of its kind, as in all our STATES BEAUTIFUL SERIES.

WALLACE NUTTING

Framingham, Massachusetts

To

J. STOGDELL STOKES

WHOSE LOVE OF THE BEAUTIFUL
ENTITLES HIM TO GENERAL REGARD

Pennsylvania Beautiful

∴

PENNSYLVANIA

I T has been thought that the charm of European life consisted in the peculiarities of custom, costume and speech to be found within the limits of a single nation, as in France. It has been counted a merit and a peculiar distinction that America is homogeneous. While we are willing to see the advantage of one speech, we believe the divergence in costumes and habits in various parts of America adds very much to the interest of the traveler. We have known more than one notable clergyman who seemed to derive advantage from his Scotch or Irish brogue. The Pennsylvanian born is quick to remark on the nasal Yankee speech and certain odd pronunciations, which latter, however, are in the best use in England. Pennsylvania has a distinct charm owing to settlements by the Swedes, Dutch, and Germans who have retained many delightful characteristics now being brought out, too late, in our literature. The peculiar branches of the Christian church found in Pennsylvania, as the Moravians or Mennonites, also give a flavor very grateful in the ordinary tameness of American life.

The architectural features of the country life of Pennsylvania, as retained from old world customs, set it apart from all other American experiences. Their wonderful barns with stone ends and overhang on one side; stone houses so often dated; post and rail fences so neatly lining their roads to this day and renewed, contrary to all economic laws; their

7

characteristic vehicles, furniture and household decorations, — all contribute
to the fascination of eastern Pennsylvania.

· The fertile, rolling lands of this part of the state are a perfect setting
for an ideal country life. We regard with highest respect the persistent
holding in one family for many generations of a home place, kept in the
pink of condition. Unquestionably this section of our country is the best
ordered part of America. True, no extensive region is without its shift-
less farmers, yet there is less of neglect and a more general pride apparent
in keeping the premises shipshape in Pennsylvania than we see elsewhere.

When we turn our attention to the great suburban district around
Philadelphia, a district which reaches out its fingers for very many miles
in some directions, we are vastly impressed by the number, the size, the
solidity, the taste, and the richness of the dwellings. Although Long
Island has developed of late years a very rich and extensive suburban
neighborhood, this is marked, sometimes, by a certain splurge, a certain
tasteless and loud type of structures, which disturb the eye and distress
the thought still more, when we consider what this means.

In Pennsylvania there has been a more careful attention to the harmo-
nizing of dwelling with country landscape. There is a quieter tone
and a better taste generally manifest in this suburban district than we
find in others. Furthermore, the stability and obvious intention of permanence conveyed by the Pennsylvania homesteads is most satisfying.
Anything which makes for peace in a country landscape is of the highest
importance, for that is what American life needs most. Anything that
makes for permanence appeals to that sense of the eternal which is so
little exemplified by modern civilization.

The Pennsylvanian has been very adroit in his study of country life.
He understands how to give the impression of a great farm as a going institution which has always been in being, although perhaps the entire es-
tablishment is comparatively recent. He seeks to avoid the impression
that he is merely a city man importing his notions into the country districts.
He has successfully studied the methods and the farmsteads of the men

DUTCH DOOR OF BARN, LEHIGH COUNTY

who have lived on the soil for many generations. While the farm build-ings may be somewhat better than those found on the average farm, they are carefully toned to convey the delightful impression of usefulness, as if the owner derived his living from the soil.

In a great many instances, also, those who have heard the call back to the land have had the good fortune or the good taste, or both, to ac-quire again the acres that were tilled by their own families, generations before. They have slightly adapted or tastefully enlarged what they found, so as to keep that charming sense of continuity which is the rarest and most desirable impression that can be afforded in rural life. The pre-vailing tints of gray or brown appeal to our historic sense. Any man who sees a comely woman in a brown gown, especially in a brown apron, at once feels that life justifies itself, and that here is the centre of home life. The Friends undoubtedly chose their gray gowns from motives of modesty and humility. However, since they were human, they could not long have remained ignorant of the fascination in soft silken gray. A dwelling, matched by barns and walls of soft brown or gray stone carries out the tone in which humanity is garbed. We feel the absolute appropriateness of the people, the dwellings, and the landscapes to one another. The best features of Germanic home life, permeated by a serene religion, have spread themselves over large areas of eastern Pennsylvania, and give a powerful impression that here a people, under sensible laws, and governed by proper ambitions, have developed a society which holds most of the features desirable and possible of attainment in country life.

We wish that the same predicate might be applied to the villages and smaller cities. In these, however, the dwellings, so generally flush with the sidewalk, have lost that retired and individual sense of cosiness which they might have obtained. Doubtless there is, more or less, a lack of aesthetic impulse in many of the villages of the district among such as think almost exclusively of material things. We feel the absence of poetry in the town.

There is, in Pennsylvania, an almost uniformly rugged and hearty

APPROACHING THE LOCK — DELAWARE CANAL

MONOCACY SHALLOWS

BELOW THE STONE BRIDGE—PERKIOMEN RIVER

A GETTYSBURG CROSSING

PIGEON BROOK BANKS

BETWEEN BUTTONWOOD BANKS—BROAD HEAD CREEK

A CROSS ROAD—NEAR PHILADELPHIA

PENNSYLVANIA BEAUTY — PERKIOMEN RIVER

THE READING LINKS

A RIPPLE IN THE BROOK—NEAR PHILADELPHIA

A LEAF STREWN DRIVE—NEAR EASTON

WISSAHICKON DECORATION

A PENNSYLVANIA HOMESTEAD—DOYLESTOWN

A LAKE BANK DRIVE—NEAR NORRISTOWN

physique. The sturdiness of the people gives an impression of capacity to overcome natural obstacles. We cannot keep from our minds the most ancient command to grow, and multiply, and fill the earth, and subdue it. The Pennsylvanian type suggests a man built for dominion over the earth. A farm is like a vigorous horse, in that it requires a steady and continuous master hand. The fickle and volatile may write books, may make music and drama. A countryside is rendered sweet and homelike only by generations of steadiness in effort. The most valuable citizen is he who has his stake in the land and has the determination to make good. This is the citizen who in the mutations of generations keeps a country from silly moods and worse vagaries. There is not a bit of anarchy in the typical Pennsylvanian. He impresses us as intending to make the most of his surroundings, and with no disposition to spurn them and to follow vague dreams and dangerous experiments. An amazingly clear setting forth of the love of the land has recently appeared in *The Lantern on the Plow*, a work referring to New Jersey, but as appropriate for Pennsylvania.

From all this it follows that the beauty of the countryside in Pennsylvania is distinct from that of other regions. It is never wild nor terrible. It is neither garish nor odd. It imparts a sense of plenty, of love for the land ingrained in the people who dwell upon it, and of their ability to make good where they are. There is no part of America where the people and the soil fit as they seem to do in Pennsylvania.

It is beyond our province to go largely into the persistence of the German speech. That phase is rapidly passing away. Meantime it has given a strong flavor to the life of the region, and inevitably certain characteristic names of pure German origin will continue. These names will establish themselves in the titles of pictures, for they are attached to many of the attractive features of Pennsylvanian life.

A very striking peculiarity of Pennsylvania is the early use and knowledge of iron. Quaint forms of household hardware and utensils are found in Pennsylvania in large numbers, and there alone. The smith was an honored personage. He remembered the lore of the Black Forest.

He shaped, in his iron, reminiscences of the Old World. This feature imparted a greater efficiency to the work of the housewife and the farm. There were utensils and devices in iron for every possible sort of work. These forms make themselves evident even outside the dwellings, and in every great kitchen. That is to say, the Pennsylvanian was not merely a farmer; he was, very often, from early times, also a metal worker. We have therefore a grafting on of metallurgy to agriculture such as to give a peculiar tone to the life of the state. Recently, of course, the wealth of the world has been poured into Pennsylvania in the tremendous development of steel. We, however, are thinking more of the earlier time, which in its use of cast and wrought iron imparted a special feature to the life of the state, before things were done so much at wholesale and before personality passed out of production.

Among the best and most delightful permanent productions of American life are the votive offerings in iron by the young man of Pennsylvania to the goddess of his affection. Until quite recent years they have not been generally known. Now, however, their appeal is broadening. The housewife also, by her needle and wheel and loom, specialized on the lines of her ancestors; and nowhere is there such a wealth of goods and gear in linen and woollen as is found in the home of an old Pennsylvanian family. The love of decoration is strongly entrenched here. While on the main lines the daughters have followed the lead of their mothers, yet the creative feeling is strong and, now and then, the theme of the past is played with pleasing modern variations. Whether we regard the external life of the farm as apparent in the fences, the barns and the dwellings, or the interior of the home, as created by the housewife, we find an intensity of love for good forms. This is the more remarkable as this trait seems singularly lacking in the smooth older life of New England, except as regards its architecture.

We observe with great delight recent literature which enshrines in a very skilful manner these fine and distinctive features of Pennsylvanian life. Such literature, by carrying the knowledge of these features of life through the country, is not only pleasing but enriching to us all.

A BLOSSOMING GABLE, ROOSEVELT BOULEVARD

There is probably a stronger local pride in Pennsylvania than is to be found in any other part of America. Particularly the proximity of New York, with its tremendous commercial development, has stimulated Pennsylvania to cherish and make much of its own local traditions.

We must think of the settlements on both sides of the Delaware River as quite similar in their origins, traditions, and customs. Often the Pennsylvanian type is also the West Jersey type. The very early settlements of the Swedes and Dutch were overlaid by the larger settlements under Penn. Thus we have, in the architecture and customs of the region, a blending of pleasing features of the better sort, which are scarcely found elsewhere in America.

In particular we cannot fail to observe the strong racial or religious motives in architecture. There is the severe plainness of the Mennonite meeting houses; the quiet but somewhat more decorative type of the

[*Text continued on page 27.*]

PENNSYLVANIA BEAUTIFUL

By Mildred Hobbs

Cool stone houses of the hills,
Bowered in the bloom of spring;
Browsing flocks of snow-white sheep;
Sweeping fields, bright-blue with flax;
Miles of green where cattle graze;
Miles of rippling, rustling corn;
Miles of tinted buckwheat bloom;
Winding rivers and canals
Where a thousand boats ply!
Great stone quarries of the hills,
Gray and ocher, red and blue;
Beds of buried ancient trees
Sparkling coal to warm the world;
Strong wide rivers, deep and long,
Where a thousand boats ply!
Alleghany's dancing blue,
The historic Delaware
Lying low among the hills,
And the lovely Susquehanna
Flowing past the tiny houses
And the mammoth bursting barns
Of the Pennsylvania Dutch
And the quiet Quaker folk;
Wooded mountains, music-filled
With the glancing falls and streams
Where the creatures of the wild
Come to drink at setting sun;
Sacred ground of Gettysburg,
Brandywine and Valley Forge!
This is Pennsylvania,
Iron-bound and beautiful!

A PENNSYLVANIA COTTAGE—NEAR PHOENIXVILLE

A COMPANIONABLE CREEK—MONTGOMERY COUNTY

THE BEAUTIFUL PERKIOMEN

A MONTGOMERY COUNTY STREAM

A PERKIOMEN OCTOBER

Friends' meeting houses; the more architecturally pretentious edifices of the Moravians with their tasteful iron work; and, last of all, the beautiful English type of the Georgian period, used in their dwellings by the Friends and other English settlers.

It is said that there were at one time in the late seventeenth century, ten thousand German emigrants waiting in a camp near London for transportation to the Delaware. These persons desired to avail themselves of the liberal charter under which Penn welcomed settlers. New England had nothing comparable to this except the little government under the inspiration of Roger Williams in Rhode Island. Too little emphasis has been placed in history on the fact that Pennsylvania, even more than New England, was a refuge from religious bigotry, and that its government was administered on broader lines of religious liberty than ever obtained in New England.

In addition to the elements already mentioned, there was also a Huguenot contingent. The Germanic strain was so strong that it dominated and still continues to dominate many Pennsylvania valleys. In New Jersey also, one of the most charming and extensive agricultural districts was named German Valley, unwisely changed during the bitterness of the late war to Long Valley.

The German habit of conserving language and custom worked in Pennsylvania against the homogeneity of the population. The persistent habit of the English of maintaining their own speech and political traditions found in the German settlers a parallel. In a new country, the population of a district being almost exclusively Germanic, many neighborhoods maintain, even to this day, a strong racial flavor. One may still meet, on Pennsylvania thoroughfares in the smaller towns, those who cannot speak English, although they are descendants of settlers who came here more than two hundred years ago.

One feature of much picturesqueness is a beehive oven, seen here and there projecting from a house end supported on corbels of masonry. We were unsuccessful in recording pictorially this charming feature. Stone watering troughs are another feature.

PENNSYLVANIA BARNS

THE ornaments on barns found in Pennsylvania, and to some small extent in West Jersey, go by the local name of hexafoos, or witch foot. They are a decoration sometimes applied on the door heads or on or about the door. They are supposed to be a continuance of very ancient tradition, according to which these decorative marks were potent to protect the barn, or more particularly the cattle, from the influence of witches. It is understood by those who are acquainted with witches that those ladies are particularly likely to harm cattle. As the wealth of the farmer was in his stock, contained in his remarkably substantial barn, the hexafoos was added to its decoration as a kind of spiritual or demoniac lightning-rod!

Candor compels the admission that these cabalistic marks on barns were a simpler and more humane measure against witches than those which were adopted in New England. If by a swastika sign on a door or a fore-bay, the power of a witch on the building concerned could be averted, there was no need of hanging the witch, and the danger of hanging some excellent old lady under wrong apprehensions was avoided. At the same time, such effects as were produced by these decorations added to the quaintness and character of the countryside. In Pennsylvania the favorite door motive on a dwelling or on the small end door of a barn, shown on page 9, is very effective. The support of these triangular door caps was secured by running the floor timbers through the walls, and extending them to the desired length where they formed the basis of the canopy. The Dutch door below is an ancient motive now copied with much gusto, not only in colonial Dutch houses but in many others where it has no place.

A variation of this motive appears on page 29, where the Black Horse tavern entrance on the old Baltimore pike is sketched. Here also we have, blended with the door head, the famous characteristic water table found

BLACK HORSE TAVERN, BALTIMORE PIKE

on the gables and the sides of many of the earlier Pennsylvania stone dwellings and, in this instance, extended to the width of a porch. (See also page 102.) Here the door head proper is arched below and supported on corbels. This really very attractive scheme is worthy of all the imitation which it has received of late years, and is commendable in that it dispenses with the posts, always annoying and always decaying. In this sketch, also, we have a good example of the cathedral chimney, that is,

TATAMY 4 MI.   DOORWAY, BETHLEHEM

the pointed Gothic arch over each chimney flue, here rising to the number of four, which is the largest number we have so far observed. The shutter downstairs is, in Pennsylvania, almost uniformly solid and panelled. The thought remains from the middle ages of using the shutter for protection from thieves, rather than as a screen against the sun. We see this solid shutter frequently on new houses in Pennsylvania. The hardware which fastens together or holds open these shutters is often quaint and elaborate. Upstairs, in the earliest examples, we frequently find the solid shutter but, sometimes as in this case, there is a lattice commonly called a blind in the North. This is, of course, wholly for protection against the sun or intrusive eyes.

The characteristic features of the barns erected by the German settlers were their stone construction, their forebays with their painted decorations which sometimes extended also to the doors on the opposite side, and to the ends. The features peculiar to theses decorations were a painted scalloped border, sometimes all about the side of the forebay, and sometimes only at the bottom, as seen on page 41. The windows were then decorated with painted arches, drops and balls, and sometimes, as on page 41, such a decoration was outlined where no window existed. But the outstanding feature most generally observed is a large circle with an inscribed star or with Gothic segmental lines. Sometimes the tracery was as intricate as that of a great Gothic rose window in a cathedral. There is an immense variation in these designs. Sometimes it is in a spiral form and again it radiates like a sunburst. The colors are always brilliant and unsparingly laid on. Time has softened the shade, but originally the effect was startlingly brilliant. According to the size of the barns, the series of wheels extends in number to six or possibly more. It often happens that the painter sought to show his skill, or to give greater interest, by varying the designs as on page 73, alternating the first with the third, the second with the fourth and so on. The six pointed star seems to be more popular than stars of other sorts. This appears on page 85, where also the effect of the forebay, open beneath, is well shown.

A four-door barn with simple decorations appears on page 61, with the smaller doors for daily use set into the great doors used only for the loads of hay or grain.

The eight pointed star seen on page 73 is a reminder of the geometric design worked out in moldings on English chests which, of course, in turn derive their inspiration from the Continent. The designs with curves, such as the second and fourth on page 73, are curiously enough seen on painted and carved boxes of about the year 1700, which boxes, however, seem to be found almost wholly in New England. There must be some exceptions to this statement, as the decoration on the boxes is plainly Frisian. We have been unable to connect the motive used on the boxes with that on the barns, but it would be rational to suppose that the furniture would be found where the barns were painted.

If, however, we take note of the painted Pennsylvania chests, we find the motives upon them to be in some cases similar to the decorations on the barns. It is very seldom, however, that the tulip design, so great a favorite on Pennsylvanian painted furniture, is seen on a barn and if so, it is always verging to some mysterious convention which leads us to wonder whether indeed it is designed to represent the tulip. The colors, however, are the same on barns and chests, because both used all the colors there were. Where, as in some instances, the decoration was carried on the end of the barn, as on page 97, it is merely to endeavor to atone for having the wooden construction instead of the stone end. Where, as on page 105, the arches of the windows interlace and are also carried over doors beneath them, the decoration becomes interestingly elaborate. The finest features of the barn decoration perhaps are, after all, not the painted work we have been describing, but the openings in the barn ends designed for ventilation, and affording no little opportunity for design. The commonest scheme is perhaps some variant of circular design, stones of a different color being used, set like spokes of a wheel around an opening. Frequently, however, there is terra cotta or brick work laid with spaces, such as we sometimes see under the porches of dwellings. A general design like the letter X is not uncommon. In instances a declension is noted by which fixed lattices of wood appear in the barn ends, outlined as windows in spacing and size.

We thought it worth while to show no less than seven variants in our pictures of these barn decorations, but even so we omit many other forms.

We are not clear as to the purpose of the forebay, which is formed by the laying of a basement wall under the wooden side of a barn so as to form an open bay, recess, or porch about five feet deep. Of course such a space afforded protection from the drip, drip of the eaves but, as it was not wide enough to protect the cattle unless they ranged themselves longitudinally along the wall, we presume it to have been a convenience to the

(*Above*) ST. PETER'S CHURCH,
LANCASTER

(*At right*) TRINITY LUTHERAN
CHURCH, READING

farmer in passing from one to another of the various doors entering the compartments behind them.

The ends of these barns were often three feet in thickness and this massive construction was continued to the eaves, at least, and often to the very peaks of the gables. This masonry is so solid that when the wood of the barns has decayed or burned, the three walls are often left intact. As one approaches a village on the south bank of the Schuylkill, near Pottstown, ruins like those of a castle appear, half covered with ivy. The author said to his companion as he rode along, "Notice that you are passing Kenilworth." Within a few rods what should we see at the road-side but the name of the village, Kenilworth, the existence of which we had been ignorant of. In this instance the barn ruins were of red sand-stone. For the most part these structures are of limestone, usually quarried on the farm itself or at a point seldom more than a mile away. The lime also, from the same rock, was burned in the immediate vicinity. A common roadside feature in Pennsylvania is an old lime kiln by the road-side, and built into a high bank, so that the loads of stone could be drawn on the upper grade to the open top of the kiln. We confess to a thorough admiration of the people who used so well the materials within their reach, adapted so thoroughly to their use. Thus the same stone burned as lime, or used in blocks, provided the entire wall structure. The pride of the farmer in his barn was further often shown not only in the decorations we have described, but by the addition of two large paintings, a horse and a cow facing one another on the side of the barn, and having between them a great American flag. Sometimes a third painting showed a sturdy cock. The farmer's name was then painted above or below all. He thus set forth his occupation and his patriotism, with naïve joy, and the name answered instead of a door plate on his dwelling. His wealth was in his barn, his cattle, and his golden sheaves, and where his treasure was, there was his heart also. As in all good farming countries, any good farmer would be ashamed if his barn were not vastly larger than his dwelling. Indeed, it was the most stinging condemnation of any man to say that his

CREEK ARCHES—THE PERKIOMEN

STATELY ARCHES—THE PERKIOMEN

A TRIBUTARY TO THE PERKIOMEN

A GOLDEN BAY—ON THE DELAWARE NEAR EASTON

DURHAM WATERS

THE PARADISE VALLEY BROOK

house was larger than his barn. It was as much as to call him impractical and extravagant and silly, and therefore on the way to ruin.

If we were to make any adverse criticism upon the dwellings of Pennsylvania, it would be that they often have a considerable height at the expense of breadth of base. That is to say, we find too many dwellings that are only one room deep, a construction, which in a house of two stories, always produces an effect of instability, lack of charm, and seems to quarrel with the otherwise substantial surroundings. One does not notice this elsewhere as much as at the outskirts of villages where a dwelling containing only one room on a floor produces an exceedingly distressing appearance. Frequently detached dwellings are constructed without windows in the sides, as if they were copied from old world houses built solidly in blocks. The absurdity of this structure in the open country is very much emphasized.

In general, however, the character of the dwellings in Pennsylvania may be fairly said to exceed in size, solidity, and general merit those seen in any other part of America. It is true that in the interior there is often lacking a fine taste and elaboration of paneling, stair, and mantel, found elsewhere. This criticism, however, is more specious than valid, for the solid and large structure has led the investigator to look for fine details within the walls. We should rather commend the builder for devoting his attention to the substantial portions of his edifice. We should not forget that these dwellings are simply farm houses and are vastly better, even in the interior, than the New England farm house. The outside is so good that we are led to the error of looking for such an interior as we could fairly expect to find only in the dwellings of persons of cultivation and wealth in the cities. We have heard the criticism that, even in the cities, the elaboration of detail found in New England, and perhaps in New York, is not usual. Our own inspection of urban dwellings has not been so extensive as to lead to any intelligent indorsement of the criticism. From our present knowledge we incline to the belief that we too often look for elaborateness where we are fortunate in finding solid simplicity.

The amazing fact is that the early Pennsylvania farmer erected a better and a larger dwelling than we find anywhere else in such numbers. The external features of these structures were rendered far more interesting by the water table on the gable. It was shingled or slated, possibly, and was a foot or two in diameter, and frequently it was repeated between the first and second story. A fine instance of this water table appears on page 65, in the old Brown house a few miles south of Quarryville, which is in turn south of Lancaster. This dwelling, with its solid lean-to having a special chimney, stepped or buttressed above the roof, is one of the most interesting of the simpler dwellings we have observed. Its wide door in the lean-to, its sheathed paneling on two floors within, its very long, large, closely set and planed floor timbers, without summer beams, a characteristic of New York and Pennsylvania construction, give us altogether a remarkable old dwelling. We notice that the original hardware also had a good deal of character, even the thumb piece of a latch being worked in the heart motive. When, as another attraction of this fine old dwelling, we add that it is one story higher on the front than on the back, where it has a grade door on the second story, that it possesses vast fireplaces of stone and mysterious crypts, we have intrigued the reader as far as we dare. To give the dwelling completion, one of the most majestic buttonwoods we have ever seen grows in front of the main door, so as, in our picture, completely to obscure it. The massiveness of this great bole seems to tell us that it and the dwelling grew together and will continue to support one another. The ancient well beneath the tree and the flagstones about, with the farm bell in the rear, complete the setting. This dwelling is some Sabbath day's journey south from the house where Robert Fulton was born, which we also show at the bottom of page 88. It is true that Fulton left here as a child, but it would seem fitting in some way to mark the spot as a memorial, even if the entire homestead is not taken over by the state and made a marine museum.

The oldest house in Lancaster County, not very far distant, is too small and simple, and too lacking in special features to be of importance.

A DECORATED BARN, LEHIGH COUNTY

The bridges of Pennsylvania give an air of age and stability to a countryside. They are generally of stone, and so are inclined to follow long, sweeping curves quite like the bridges in Spain. We never tire of their fascination.

The bridge over the Delaware at Washington's Crossing is unhappily not of this sort but, as he was obliged to use boats, the matter is not so important.

We noticed a bridge somewhat northeast of Lebanon, in which the central stone containing the names of the builders and their date was precisely the shape of an arch topped tombstone, as if it had been set in the wall to make it more permanent. We understand this stone is shortly to be destroyed by the widening of the bridge. Modern silos of stone are an added feature of architectural permanence.

The community of Ephrata is one of those features of Pennsylvania life which has attracted a great deal of attention, perhaps owing to its unusualness. The quaint old buildings, a sketch of which we show on page 125, and the interesting community which existed at Ephrata and which has for the most part passed away, are set forth in a little book on

[*Text continued on page 52.*]

THE BRANDYWINE BATTLE SITE

Written for picture on page 45 by MILDRED HOBBS

Soft clouds of leaning April willows shine
Like silver gauze upon the mirrored stream;
The springtime breezes play their happy theme
Through budding trees along the Brandywine;
And on the river's ragged banks recline
Contented cattle sent to browse and dream
Among the violets; and grasses gleam
Like points of flickering fire upon a shrine.

Fair trees, deep-rooted in a bloodied sod,
New life absorbed from sacrifice divine,
And pleasant pastures of historic fame,
Long may your beauty breathe the peace of God!
O blood-red waters of the Brandywine,
How crimson are your pools of sunset-flame!

THE SKIPPACK IN OCTOBER

A STROUDSBURG BROOK

NEAR DURHAM FURNACE

BRANDYWINE BATTLE SITE

THE END OF AUTUMN—NEAR PHILADELPHIA

A PERKIOMEN NOOK

A CURVING LANE—NEAR VALLEY FORGE

DELAWARE BANKS—NEAR EASTON

THE CREEK IN MAY—NEAR VALLEY FORGE

A BROOK—MONTGOMERY COUNTY

DREAM LANE

Written for picture on page 47 by MILDRED HOBBS

Little bird-enchanted lane
Leading down to Valley Forge,
Tell us of the long ago!
Did he pass along your way,
The father of our country,
Pausing here beneath the blossoms hanging low
To pray
To the God of nature's peace and love and beauty?
As he lingered here and listened
To the brooklet running gold
Over singing stones that glistened
In the sun
Was he told
That his battles would be won?
Little lane, bird-enchanted,
In a winding such as this
Where the trees and meadows bloom and waters gleam
Did he dream
Of a glorious republic?
How he suffered with his patriots
Through bitterness of winter,
Waiting long,
And patiently holding to his heart the vision
Of a nation free and strong!
Valley Forge where men and boys
Bleeding, starving and exhausted, bravely fell —
And not in vain!
But the tragedy and pain —
Little lane,
If you could only tell!

The Ephrata Cloister. The edifices make no pretention to architectural merit. They are peculiar only in that they include within them all the appurtenances for an independent existence. The people of this community made practically everything that they possessed. Their culinary and textile utensils and apparatus are of very great interest. A great many of the utensils have been sold but now a stop has been put to such sales, and the things that remain are well worth seeing. The simple faith and pure life of these people is a pleasant memory. The fact that in Pennsylvania they were welcome to develop according to their special tenets speaks well for the largeness of spirit already accorded by the government of that state from the first.

The life of the community in its cloister resembled the monastic. While marriage was not impossible it was not thought to be conducive to the highest spiritual state, and only that portion of the community that remained single were residents in the brothers' or in the sisters' edifice. This Seventh Day Baptist organization continued the use of the German tongue, published theological and other works, and has left a strong impress on the life of the state. On page 289 we show the tombstone of Bruder Philemon, one of the oldest in the cemetery.

The idea of a Protestant cloister, carried out in the lives of these people resembles, in some particulars at least, the communities of Shakers in Maine, New Hampshire, and New York. It is an interesting phase of American colonial life which gives a strong flavor to the rural districts of Pennsylvania. We would not give the impression that the activities of the Seventh Day Baptists have ceased in Pennsylvania. In Waynesborough there is a flourishing church. There is another at Salemville. At Nunnery in Franklin County there is an interesting old graveyard, now used for general interments. It contains the grave of Peter Lehman, the supposed founder of the Snow Hill Institute.

The date of this society's activities in America is early. The religious institution of Ephrata was founded about 1730.

Ephrata is a pilgrimage point for tourists. We regard with great re-

A FINE OLD CHESTER DWELLING

spect the conscientious devotion of the founders of its peculiar organization, and enjoy the strong relish of the quaint customs and simple living handed down through them. For instance, to mention only one point, the cloister dwellers slept with wooden pillows on bare boards, to mortify the body. They objected to the intrusion of civil government and were sustained in their religious position by Washington. An interesting episode was the visit of Peter Miller, one of the early worthies of this organization, to Washington, in behalf of a Tory spy who was condemned under the laws of war. Washington informed Miller that nothing could be done for the spy. "Friend," exclaimed Miller, "he is the worst enemy I have." "Then," said Washington, "how can you ask for his pardon?" Whereupon Miller, with tears in his eyes, replied, "My Savior did as much for me." The spy was pardoned because of Miller's meek, forgiving spirit, and the episode was commemorated in a poem. In the history of religions we find, here and there, men of the utmost devotion who are, perhaps, more or less handicapped by peculiar customs which have no necessary connection with character.

A RURAL PARADISE

WE think this name fairly applicable to Wayne County. With its hundred lakes, its mountains and deep valleys, its numerous streams and falls, its farms like eyries, overlooking valleys of peace, it has a delight in store for all those who love to roam in the real country. In populous Pennsylvania Wayne County's largest town, Honesdale, has only two or three thousand people, though the solidity of its dwellings, the beauty of its square and the Hollandlike aspect of its river flowing through the town give the impression of a large and beautiful centre. As the old terminus of a great canal, it probably looked forward to greater commercial development, which happily did not come, or has gone. As one stands on its bridge and faces the great cliff overlooking the town, he derives an impression that he stands in a secluded valley of beauty, a kind of miniature American Vale of Cashmere. Here in a hostelry covered with ivy and looking out on churches of stone, one feels apart from those raw roadside taverns so characteristic of most of the state. The dear little river all up and down the valley poses for its picture at every turn. The fine green slopes call one to the wide, free visions to be had from their summits. The elm tree, which does not show at its best in the more southern sections of Pennsylvania, gives a real New England aspect to Wayne and Susquehanna counties. Indeed, the height, the contour and the vegetation of Wayne County very strongly suggest Vermont. If we pause to remember that the hills of both regions are a part of the same Appalachian system, we shall understand better the similarity.

The paucity of lakes in some parts of Pennsylvania seems to be fully

ON THE DELAWARE CANAL—NEAR EASTON

A STREAM—NEAR AMBLER

BELOW THE WATER GAP

COBB'S CREEK—PHILADELPHIA

VALLEY FORGE

A WISSAHICKON POOL

MAY ON THE WISSAHICKON

atoned for in this county. The attraction of these lakes is the greater, that they are not yet surrounded with the tawdry dwellings so character- istic of American watering places. In fact, most of them are hidden away in the hills and are entirely unappropriated.

There is a charm in such landscapes which could not, by old methods of conveyance, be fully appreciated. In the old days, when it was neces- sary for a weary horse to drag one toilsomely to the higher slopes, hill homes were handicapped in their enjoyment, but now the new methods of locomotion make nothing of these grades, and one swiftly arrives at a vantage point from which the delights of the long, deep valley with its silver stream are opened to us. This region is the perfection of location for fruits. The peculiar appeal to us just now is this: we have here the last available eastern county of Pennsylvania to be possessed by the lovers of landscape beauty. It is a little too far from great cities to be the dwell- ing of those who must every day go to town. Here, therefore, for a very modest sum, one who loves the country may become possessed of a site as perfect as one could wish, for health, for outlook, for land available to produce the wealth of the hills. For here, even in Pennsylvania, we see quite occasionally an abandoned farm. It is seldom that one observes in this country the great solid substantial homesteads seen in more southern regions of the state. It has in the past been too difficult to go to and re- turn from market. There is many a wonderful, strategic location decorated by the beauty of trees, backed by mighty hills, descending by far winding roads to the distant towns and altogether alluring and satisfactory. Con- sider that here is a county with more than twenty towns — and fewer than thirty thousand people. We are far from every annoyance, on many of these roads, of poles, wires, noise, dust, and the multitudinous horrors of a crowded civilization. We have never felt any temptation to become the lords of domains in the broad, fertile lowlands. But here is a little kingdom on every hillside which rouses every old hankering after the land, that remains in the old Adam. Our fingers itch and our brains tingle to get at work upon one of these tempting hill farms. For be it known, this is not a kingdom of rough, rocky land. There are fine, fertile fields or areas which may be made so, on every farm. There are materials at hand for permanent dwellings which may embody every modern comfort and every ancient charm.

We do not know how long it will be before the farseeing will carry out the almost universal love for a country home, at once protected and sightly, such as is to be found in this wonderful county. It can be only a question of a short generation before the merits now overlooked will be sought and cherished and developed. Once let the tide of improvement begin, and this county may easily become the first in the state for ideal development.

Susquehanna County is, in part, on the main track of north and south travel. It shares with Wayne County some of the merits which we have been describing, of which elsewhere.

Wayne is evidently a poets' and theologians' county. These names, scarcely believable, are actually villages marked on the map: in the north, Autumn Leaves, Starlight, and Hiawatha; and in the south, Angels. The Moosic range in this county rises to the dignified height of twenty-five hundred feet, so that the reader may see that our ecstasy in regard to these sharp rising hills is borne out by the statistical elevations. That the settlers really thought themselves in a land of milk and honey is seen in such names as Galilee, Bethany and Damascus.

THE SUSQUEHANNA

SO long ago that we do not care to reckon it, an old steel engraving hung on the walls of our boyhood home "Hunting on the Susquehanna." It has been one of our ambitions to follow this stream in its upper reaches. In general it may be said that the nearer we approach its mouth, the less interesting does it become. We may have occasion, in another volume, to record some of its aspects in its wide western sweep.

QUADRUPLE BARN DOORS

Following it upward in its eastern and northern branches, through the counties of Luzerne, Lackawanna, Bradford and Susquehanna, we have learned to love it more and more as we reach its narrower windings. We overlook the dereliction of the stream in slying away out of the state to flirt with New York. After all, it is faithful, for the most part, to Pennsylvania. From its first meanderings between Wayne and Susquehanna Counties, we have shown it in this volume at Starrucca, Susquehanna, Hickory Grove, Hallstead, Tunkhannock, Wilkes-Barre, Shickshinny and other points. There are, indeed, sections where mining has rendered it no longer beautiful. A companion, seeing ducks swimming in water laden with fine black coal dust, suddenly remarked that he saw now where the egg coal came from! We are obliged to have coal, and we would not be found among those constantly twitting on the unloveliness which inevitably accompanies the mining of this element, which is really the great national boon of Pennsylvania to the world. We are bound to state, also, that when we consider the vast quantities of coal mined, we are gratified to find, very near the centres of this enterprise, rural beauties of the highest merit, such as may be found in the ride from Nanticoke, a little below Wilkes-Barre, to Tunkhannock, and various regions northeast, north, and northwest of that place. Sometimes one has merely to go over one rise of land from a blackened coal centre, to find oneself in a countryside as quiet, sweet and perfect as could be found in a state where no coal exists.

Some confusion arises from the various names given to the contributary streams of the Susquehanna. Thus we have the East Branch, the North Branch, etc., the main streams coming together at Sunbury, whence southerly the river is so large and broad as to become majestic. To our thought a subordinate stream such as appears in "A Perfect Day," page 294, or in "The Young Susquehanna," page 274, is more pleasurable to view, or at least to picture, than the broader effects such as are seen at Nanticoke, page 282.

Susquehanna County contains much fine scenery, as on the Great Bend, page 274, and as on the Susquehanna river, page 293, which passing on the great trunk line to Binghamton and the north, one sees at the right.

The village of Montrose, and in fact various towns in this northeast corner of the state, present a park-like effect since their dwellings stand well back from the highway, and are beautifully ornamented with trees.

New Milford has become a considerable center for guests. In parts it is very attractive. No doubt in time, Wayne County, which is not far away, will derive similar benefits from the discoveries that will be made there in the next decade.

WYOMING AND LACKAWANNA COUNTIES

IT is difficult to comprehend that these counties alone contain perhaps greater mineral wealth than the entire kingdom of Italy. Pennsylvania, in fact, is the finest example the world holds of a region rich in all the essentials of a modern civilization. The magnificent farmlands

A LEHIGH COUNTY HOMESTEAD

come to the bases of the mountains, which contain the sinews of peace and war. Considered broadly, as compared with many American states, and many foreign countries, Pennsylvania alone is not only an empire, but a mother of empires. It is scarcely given to any other region on earth to be endowed with lands rich like the prairie states, hills of iron and coal, streams of wonderful beauty, and sweet, remote uplands of pastoral simplicity, decorated with the finer trees of the temperate zone. Wilkes-Barre and Scranton are beautiful modern cities, and though they live on coal, they are utilizing their immediate environment by parking river-banks and uplands. Going out from these cities to the southeast, one comes into the famous Pocono resorts, and to the northwest, the stream- and lake- and mountain-regions and remote farms are still as unspoiled as they were a hundred years ago. A stream coming down from the north into Nanticoke forms what in the west we should call a cañon. It has in places very bold and picturesque crags rising by the side of the road, which in turn follows the creek. We should, by the way, be very careful to say creek, as the word "brook" is unfamiliar in this state, and indeed anywhere in America beyond New England, although we love the word and it is common in England. Anything in this region smaller than a river is a creek, and there seems to be no synonym for the word except "stream," or "branch."

The outstanding attraction in this region is, however, Kitchen Creek. Under the wise control of a hunting and fishing club, it has been protected from unpleasing exploitation. There is an utter absence of objectionable features on the highway where one begins the journey on foot to the falls, and throughout the entire ramble.

There is a long series of cascades or waterfalls, some of pretentious elevation, and others of that minor descent fitted to please the heart of the boy which remains in every man, and remind him of the miniature dams and water-wheels that were his delight. The conformation of the rock a little below the highway reminds one almost of the honey-comb. The cliff at the falls themselves is broken away or worn in those uncouth anomalous shapes which have always had a fascination not only for this age, but for remote and uncivilized man. Here the inevitable visionary who can point out faces in the rock may find his paradise. Probably all of our presidents, together with numberless other great man of the past, have their noses or eyes or some portion of their facial anatomy still carved in the rock. We have not, in all our ramblings, seen a deep forest dell surpassing in natural beauty the various windings of Kitchen Creek. We have only to refer the reader to " An Untamed Wood," page 271, and to the pictures on pages 272, 273, 279 and 282, to bear out our statement that here is a variety of beautiful forms of the highest merit. Where would one discover a more oddly charming combination than appears in " A Squirrel Bridge," page 269, or in " A Pennsylvania Dell," page 268? In places, the valley of the brook spreads to present a spacious forest canopy. Again it narrows, and the rushing waters leap down their enmossed crags. Dainty shoots arise on the shelves of the rocks. At the very brink of the stream majestic boles of the black birch have taken their stand. One is much astonished to find these great trees, some of them two feet and a half in diameter, and rising like Egyptian pillars into the dim temple heights above. This tree is what is sometimes called the mahogany birch. Alternating with it one finds beautiful beeches and evergreens.

A feature of very striking interest is the flagstone path which extends

THE OLD BROWN HOUSE, LANCASTER COUNTY

wherever needed for a great distance along the borders of the stream. Apparently most of these natural flags were picked from the bed of the stream itself. In places, they are piled across a little gorge to a considerable height. Again, as at one of the more beautiful falls (on the left, page 259) they are built into a stair of stone, which in its curving line and its finely chosen setting, matches the most cunning art of the landscape gardener. Yet all is free and natural and wild. The number of the falls, little and big, is so great that we lost count, since there are numerous drops of a foot or two over old logs or ledges. These we passed between the more marked and striking cataracts, some of which must have been appropriate abodes for the gods of the waters worshiped by the aborigines.

It would be entirely possible to record this region, which is about two miles in extent, and without overdoing it, by one or two hundred pictures.

While the falls themselves are perhaps not more beautiful than those at Winona, Buck Hill, Bushkill, and their compeers, the paths that lead along Kitchen Creek present superior charms, because they are so extensive and various. While to the eye some of the cascades which were more abrupt might have surpassed it, we think that pictorially speaking " A Forest Stair," page 279, is perhaps as beautiful in effect as any.

It would be difficult to overemphasize the pleasure which we felt in finding all this beauty unmarred by man. We might revise the poet's line in regard to this dreamy vale so as to run, " Where every prospect pleases, and man's himself worth while."

We were greeted at the parking space by a caretaker who asked us where we learned of this secluded spot. He seemed to express some surprise that a traveler from a distance should know anything of it. It is apparently not the purpose of those who control the approaches to blaze abroad these secret beauties. Possibly these gentlemen will not thank us for this so public expatiation on the subject. But we shall certainly do all American citizens a good turn by saying that if they start on this tramp some hours before a refection is required, since there is nothing to eat hereabouts, and if they are interested in what nature has prepared to show us with the least possible assistance from man, they will find it here, and find it in paths so still, except for the rustling of the leaves and the babbling of the stream, that they might easily be in the original wilds.

MONROE AND PIKE COUNTIES

PIKE COUNTY lies fair upon the Delaware. It is really a nose thrust in between New Jersey and New York, Port Jervis being a corner town for three states. The beauties of the upper Delaware, in Wayne and Pike Counties, show here bold cliffs and sharp ascents, and there broad lowlands and splendid bordering meadows. Bushkill Creek is on the

[Text continued on page 72.]

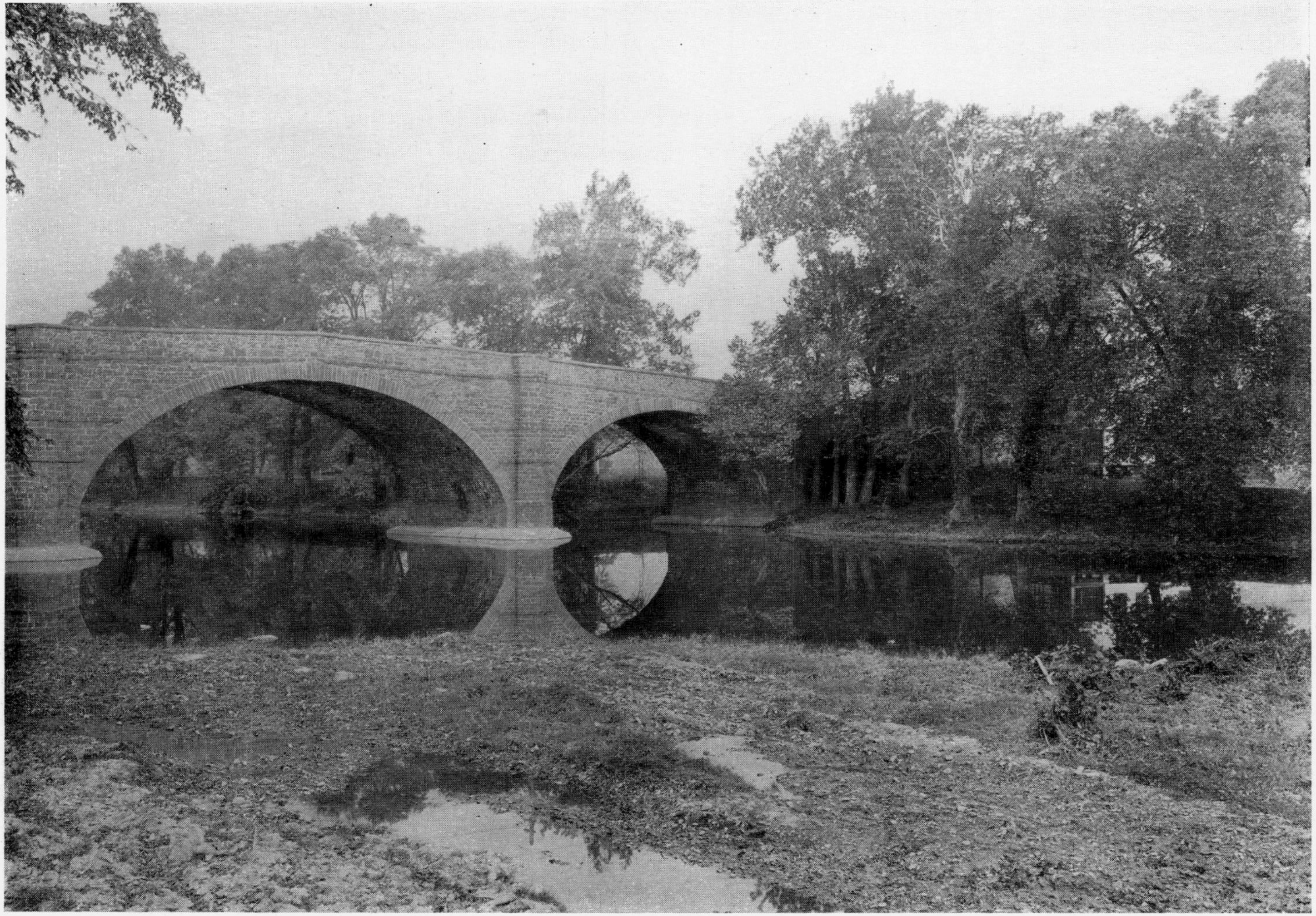

A PERKIOMEN BRIDGE

HOME BLOSSOMS—NEAR PHILADELPHIA

STREAM LINES—THE PERKIOMEN

THE HARVEST FIELD—BUCK COUNTY

A DURHAM POOL

AN ANCIENT KITCHEN—CHESTER

IN AUTUMN

Written for picture on page 69 by MILDRED HOBBS

Have you ever wandered through a brown field of stubble
Sending out the pungent odor of the early fall,
Scattered with the glory of the heaped-up pumpkins,
Each one gleaming like a great golden ball?

Have you ever listened there when the light breezes
Touched the tassels bending from the tall stacks of corn
Spreading out their ragged ribbon-robes among the harvest,
Clear against the cool sky of an autumn morn —

Whispering together as the wind ran through them,
Rustling the drying husks and the dead vines
Of the golden pumpkins and the green and yellow squashes
Piled into pyramids in long shining lines?

Have you felt the rhythm and the harmony of autumn —
Birches and maples in a crimson-orange blaze,
Trees bending low with their red and russet apples,
And the skies filling with a soft smoky haze?

Bronze leaves, scarlet leaves whirling in a circle,
Purple-clustered grapes, and a leaping brush fire,
Birds wheeling southward, a lone cricket chirping!
Oh, has it filled you with a maddening desire

To hold it, to keep it from the cold clutch of winter,
The pomp and the glory and the beauty of it all?
Like a rich robe for the last long dreaming
Is the gorgeous raiment of the earth in the fall!

bounds between Pike and Monroe counties. To the north and east of it are numerous hidden lakes, narrow serpentine streams, and several water-falls, like Dingman's, which is perhaps the best known. Pike County is another of the rural portions of Pennsylvania which is doubtless destined to very much larger development as the seat of country estates.

THE POCONO REGION

MONROE COUNTY, in its upper section, is practically synonymous with the Pocono region. At first it is disappointing in that the general contour is that of a table land. We are at the greatest elevations, without having a sense of the fact, and there is a certain bareness here and there, arising no doubt from the windswept nature of the location. As soon, however, as one goes a little apart into the nooks and valleys, one discovers a large number of streams, which surprise one at every turn by their varying moods. Here they follow luxuriant evergreens; there they skirt along by the poplars, whose little hands are eternally beckoning us. At the next turn we may come upon majestic buttonwoods, with their great leaves suggesting the tropics, and their brown and green and gray trunks, which indicate that whatever the style and color, they mean always to be the fashionable tree of the wood. The walnut or the shagbark, which is here the more common variety, is found by the roadsides and lanes and by the ledges of the pastures. There is frequently observed, as on the way to Paradise Falls, a long, sloping ledge of rock, over which a sheet of water glides silently but rapidly. We think it unnecessary to refer spe-cifically to all the illustrations of these features. The reader will find them set forth in many examples.

The Poconos are the nearest very high land to Philadelphia, and they are the natural resort for those whose time is limited. Furthermore, there have been built up here several institutions of a distinctive character, which socially or morally or otherwise have gained prestige, and are maintaining

A LEHIGH COUNTY BARN

the region as a strong magnet to those who are drawn by such considerations, and who is not?

The principal charm of the Poconos consists of the water features. There are numerous falls delightful to explore. The Buck Hill falls, consisting of a series of successive leaps, are so situated as to be easily accessible. The quite different character of the upper and lower falls renders each more attractive by contrast. The beautiful bowl into which the lower falls drop provides a little water amphitheater decorated with moss and lichen. It is such a spot as Horace or Ovid would have loved, and concerning which they would have given us some of their charming odes. We have shown the lower fall in various aspects, and are especially happy to show one of the upper cascades. The dell below the falls is deep, shady, and massed with foliage so as to afford a cool retreat in the hottest days of summer.

Above the falls also the stream is delightful with rapids and pools, and a wise use has been made of the waters and the banks by the bridges and paths.

Perhaps the most beautiful fall in Pennsylvania, at least in its appeal to us, is the Indian Ladder. While its beauty may be seen from afar on the banks of the cañon-like cavity into which it drops, its appearance from that point is insignificant in comparison with the view close at hand. Its openness to the light of day is one of its merits. Some minds shrink from the dark and deep misty crevasses into which falls like the Bushkill cast themselves. Here, at the Indian Ladder, there is sunshine, and no sense of being shut away. The three principal steps of the fall, turning like the wind of a stair, the fine outlines of the cliffs, the dainty arrangement of the foliage, and the unsophisticated air of the entire valley, are felt as an accumulated and supremely beautiful general impression. We have thought so highly of this scene that we have used it on the jacket of this volume.

The fall is to be visited only on foot, for the last half mile or so, but there is nothing difficult in the journey, which is thoroughly pleasurable, especially if undertaken with a congenial companion. There are aspects of beauty, each most appealing, as one approaches the fall from the rapids below. The writer had the misfortune to slip on a mossy rock in the midst of the stream, smashing some of the bones of his instrument, if not his own, and he is therefore particularly gratified that even after what promised to be a serious disaster, he still brought away these images of beauty. The fall is very happily named, and it is to be hoped that its freedom from exploitation may continue.

The Winona falls, though situated at some distance from the Indian Ladder, can scarcely be passed by by one who loves mountain waters. There is a succession of these falling torrents — seven, we believe, each differing sufficiently from its companions to add to our interest. Indeed, comparison gives beauty most of its charm. Some of these falls are in locations surrounded by massive and bold cliffs, and miniature suspension

BUSH KILL FALL

AN UPPER WINONA FALL

A WILKES BARRE BROOK

UPPER BUCK HILL

A POCONO TERRACE

A POCONO RAPID

A WEE BROOK—LANCASTER COUNTY

STEPS OF FOAM—WINONA FALLS

WINONA CENTRAL FALL

POPLAR RAPIDS—POCONO MOUNTAINS

LEVIS FALLS

LANCASTER DECORATIONS

bridges, and heavily banked foliage. They are, it is true, commercialized, but no objectionable features have intruded upon the waters themselves. The stroll to the uppermost fall is not difficult although there is not a little climbing of stairs. It is a peculiar delight to find such a succession of beauties hidden here among the hills, and we are led to wonder why such natural attractions are so infrequent. We know nothing of the kind among the White Mountains. We must attribute these pleasing phenomena to the peculiar geologic formation and to the abundance of rain on these slopes.

The Bushkill fall is altogether the most impressive, from its solemn and awful depths, its seclusion and its dense mists, from the steep approaches and the roar with which it dashes itself to the mystic pool below. The principal leap is impressively high, and in the springtime, when the waters are abundant, one feels, standing below, a sense of awe, and just that sufficient thrill of danger which we humans love. Below the main falls are subordinate cascades in this sheer abyss between the hills. While we recommend a visit in the spring, if one desires to get an impression of mystery and grandeur, and would even recommend a stormy day for enhancing these impressions, we cheerfully record the gentler and sweeter impressions imparted by the thinner veil of water on a brilliant day in midsummer. The greens here are superb, the conifers seeming to predominate. To see this fall, however, in all its moods, one should not miss an autumn visit, on a day of blue skies and rolling white clouds. With such an upper background, with the gorgeousness of the reds and browns and yellows against the blue, with the superb rock colorings and contours, and the music of the waters, we are in the presence of nature when she fairly overcomes us by her beauty and variety. At such times we are easily able to understand how the ancients, without other revelations, were led to worship. But even so, oriental peoples, like the Chinese, make the love of a landscape an act of worship, and find an inspiration in it which is only an occasional mood with us occidentals. We go to places like the Buck Hill falls, look, leave, and forget. The Chinese, at least among their men of education, spend an hour almost daily, in a really ecstatic state, in watching the sky's splendors suspended above their gardens, where evergreens and waters are taught to simulate the grander features of wild regions.

Whether or not Americans in numbers will ever come to lose themselves for long in the intriguing beauty of such views as this before us, we do not know. But we could easily imagine a life surrounded by such inspirations, led on to fine achievements of the mind. Strangely, it is said that most great literary productions have originated in attics, which were cold or hot or wretchedly furnished. It is probably true that most works of genius, as we name them, have been forced, or at least induced, by hunger or cold. Might there not be a far finer florescence of genius, were creative minds to place themselves at strategic points among the hills, where the beckonings of sky fingers and the celestial combinations of cliff and foliage and meadow and stream formed the foreground?

The Paradise falls afford another and quite different appeal. The swift glide of the stream over the ledges for a long distance before the final leap; the breaking up of the waters below, that leap among the boulders; the turn of the stream at this point; and the secondary cascade; the great beauty of the surrounding trees, of many varieties of leaf and stem; altogether afford a fascinating experience well worth two journeys, each to fill a day.

The delight of our minds in the play of waters is happily not confined to the more notable streams and falls. Little mountain becks and burns unnamed, often unseen, and mostly unappreciated, appeal to another side of our nature. We begin to feel the lure of personal possession in a small cascade. We wish to decorate its banks and to clear it of broken branches, and to provide a little Forest of Arden, each one for ourselves. In appropriating a small cascade, such as that on page 161, to our own peculiar love and communion, we have no sense of selfishness, since the very solitariness of the spot indicates that others have passed it by, uncaring. This felicity, arising out of the charming water play even

ON THE BORDER OF BUCKS COUNTY

of a small brook, is too much overlooked by Americans. There are probably thousands of little dells in America which, in Japan, China, or India
would form nuclei of famous country estates. Those past masters of
landscape gardening, those minds, fellowshiping, apparently by nature,
with the world of beauty, would create miniature Gardens of Eden where
now the human foot seldom treads.

Paradise Valley, which comes down on one side of the Poconos, and
opens at length a little north of Stroudsburg, has as its center a stream
with so many moods of beauty that we hardly know where to find its like.
While there are no great surging leaps of the waters, there are so many
rapids and eddies, there are so many deep banks over which the dainty
evergreens of spring, with their parti-colored fingers, reach, there are so
many noble buttonwoods laving their water, seeking roots in the banks,

that we may find here solace for days. Many small bridges afford vantage points for viewing the stream. We do not know whether fishermen find much here to their liking, but in the soft bordering meadows and in small orchards and cottages, and in the freshly opening aspects of beauty that meet one as he passes around the angles of the hills, there is an enriching of the heart and a sufficient appeal to the emotions.

One is often saddened by observing the sort of events that are required to arouse interest in some minds. It would appear that certain persons require a great shock to become interested. Certain others will travel across the country for the welter of pleasure that they derive from seeing two men fight. No small proportion of men and women have been observed to sit for days at a time within a stone's throw of natural beauties of the highest type, without any apparent interest in life beyond a game. A novel may be interesting, sometimes, we think, in proportion to its horrible, its repulsive, or its unnatural features. Yet we believe that there is, deep in the heart of man, an approval of and a delight in perfection of form. We believe that in the end the finer attractions may make their appeal. Just now a person of fine taste and intelligence who stands at the delivery desk of a public library and notices the titles that go out, spreading their turgid, malodorous stream through our commonwealths, must feel a shudder of fear at the sort of appeal required to interest mankind.

In all our journeys amongst the beauty spots of Pennsylvania, we were almost always alone. At the Buck Hill falls, by the side of a great concourse of guests, we did naturally find persons scanning the loveliness which nature had unveiled. But at other points in Pennsylvania, in spring, summer, or autumn, on mountain or in meadow, by fall or stream, we have almost never encountered an individual looking at a landscape. The same, with the exception of those natural features everywhere talked about, and in the height of the season, is true in other states. The only spot in Maine where we have seen anyone looking at a landscape was at Mount Kineo. In New Hampshire we found a few persons at the Flume, not, by the

A FESTOONED LANE—POCONO MOUNTAINS

BEYOND THE STREAM—NEAR PHILADELPHIA

THE ROBERT FULTON BIRTHPLACE—LANCASTER COUNTY

INDIAN LADDER FALLS

A HAPPY CHOICE—NEAR PHILADELPHIA

A BRIDAL JUNE—POCONO MOUNTAINS

way, one of the most interesting points in that state, and on Mount Washington. For the rest, nobody was looking at anything. We would not be misunderstood. We know that millions of persons at times do enjoy the natural world. We take to ourselves no special merit for quality of mind and heart that is better than that possessed by the multitude, but we are stating the fact, that in our roamings at all seasons, we have as a rule been left in solitary enjoyment of the most entrancing objects which our search of years could discover.

We would say that those who visit the Poconos would do best to follow up Paradise Valley to reach the summit. This region and the little neighborhood of Canadensis, and the side roads and valleys, are very rich in blossom time.

The Levis fall is quite accessible. It requires so brief a time to visit any of these cascades that we think it is a mistake to omit them, although we found very few of the habitués of the Poconos who had seen them all (page 82).

At about the point of junction of Bear Creek and the Todyhanna at Stoddardsville, in the edge of Luzerne County but fairly in the Pocono district, the Lehigh river falls over a most picturesque series of steps. This fall, in the spring of the present year, was carrying a great volume of water, and without qualification shows greater variety and mass than any other of the falls in the entire district. It is happily directly on the roadside. We show two aspects of it, the principal one being on page 171. This fine cascade may be viewed from various angles, and in this particular is different from most of the falls in the Pocono. It lies in the open, in a most charming locality. A little below it there is the wreck of an old mill of stone. The light coming through the windows, and the configuration of the ruin in general, suggests a castle. We have seen no spot so well fitted for development as a private estate, with a water feature close at hand. The ride, indeed, from Wilkes-Barre to the Poconos through this point instead of by way of Scranton, brings into view many pleasing land-

[*Text continued on page 93.*]

INDIAN LADDER FALLS

Written by MILDRED HOBBS for picture on page 89

Where rapid waters foam and glide
Over the Pocono mountain-side,

Falling, plunging, beating their way
Among the rocks smooth-worn with spray,

One sees fleet-footed warriors leap
The boulders of the craggy steep

With graceful birchen barks and packs
Borne swiftly on their supple backs.

Against the silver of the stream
Their brilliant painted feathers gleam,

And in the music of the falls
One hears the echo of their calls.

Beautiful Indian Ladder, white
With fountains in a foamy flight!

Great glistening steps whose crystal lights
Lure on to hidden mountain heights,

Your waters sing the days of old
When Red-skins wandered free and bold

Over America's hills and streams—
How glad, how sad is your song of dreams!

DAVID RITTENHOUSE BIRTHPLACE, MONTGOMERY CO.

scapes, several of which we have recorded. "A Shadowed Ribbon Road,"
page 100, shows a little side way of much charm. Somewhat beyond this
picture we see "The Shadow Dell," page 111.

THE WATER GAP

THE Delaware, winding between the hills, perhaps we should say
mountains, and dividing New Jersey from Pennsylvania, has at
length cut its way down to such a level that, its work being done, it may
glide along leisurely and reflect the crests which it has conquered. The
Water Gap is famous everywhere, and deservedly, though we think that the
Susquehanna below Wilkes-Barre is almost as good. It would be dangerous, lest we arouse the hostility of local partisans, to compare the Water
Gap with the Highlands of the Hudson. In one particular, New York is
now ahead of Pennsylvania in the carrying out of its scenic mountain highways. We found it almost impossible, owing to fringes of trees, to obtain
satisfactory outlooks upon the Water Gap. We confess ourselves astounded
when informed that the mountains of the Gap rise above two thousand
feet. There is no adequate measure of dimensions, so that one is much
deceived. Stroudsburg is a natural point of meeting and departure, per-

haps the most notable in eastern Pennsylvania north of Philadelphia. One goes from here into those parts of the Pocono Mountains whose chief attraction is their quiet evergreen forests, and their dignified, retired summer homes. One goes also up the Paradise Valley and along the upper Delaware toward Port Jervis, a drive which, for long, rolling sweeps and broad meadows with distant hills, is of a very high order. One goes also by way of the river around the Kittatinny Range, to Bangor, Easton, and the South. Another route, leaving out the Water Gap but by way of the Wind Gap, through Saylorsburg to the south, is a very satisfactory drive.

A journey undertaken to follow the Delaware wherever available by steam, or otherwise by canoe, from its far upland waters to the vicinity of Easton, is one to be undertaken by persons who have that happy faculty of carrying through the investigation of a particular region. A series of pictures of the Delaware alone, in all its moods, and from youth to maturity, should be an achievement and an occupation sufficiently engrossing while it was being attained. Such projects carried through leave one afterwards with a various stock of valuable experiences and memories, together with the records which recall all these. With it all there may go an increased springiness of the gait, an enlargement of the chest measure, an enriching of the heart, and a general sanity and poise. Indeed, we know nothing comparable with undertaking to explore a certain district of a state, noting by pen and otherwise its striking or pleasing features. That strength in statement and accuracy of estimate which forms a well-developed character is in no way better secured than by an independent investigation out of doors of something that has not been well done as yet. It is ever, or should be, a delight to be recommended, to discover something not hitherto observed. Our own occupations have forbidden leisurely and thorough work of such a nature, but for youth or age of either sex, we can think of nothing more conducive to the good of the country investigated, and to the good of the investigator, than the devotion of oneself to some such object.

What we may call a geographic sense, lacking any better term, which has been so nobly encouraged to develop, through the *Geographical Magazine*, that monumental and superb accomplishment, adds immensely to the joy of living. To be able to place oneself, in one's thought, in the world, all the time; that is, to feel one's situation in regard to the mountains and valleys and cities, to see, as we rest before we sleep, the panoramas of counties opening before us, to leap in our thought from crest to crest, and to note the sources of wealth and the decorations of a state, and to be conscious always of one's position in a landscape, even as a bird that flies, — all this is something not difficult of attainment, but immensely satisfactory. Doubtless it is to be assisted by aviation. One would say, however, that in that mode of movement, there should be greater interest and instruction in circling back and forth over a single valley until one learned it, than in shooting across states and acquiring only transitory impressions.

We have to confess our envy of the aviator. He is able to secure those panoramas impossible to one on the ground. He absorbs at one glance the salient features of a county. To him a river is an instant and complete magnificence. The lakes are scattered like mirrors of the gods. Scarcely do the mountains frame his picture. He moves from one watershed to another while we are thinking of it. He has in our generation suddenly attained to many of the attributes which we had counted as belonging exclusively to superhuman intelligence. He is said to have conquered the air, but the victory is over the earth. Whether we shall ever live to achieve a volume of airplane visions we do not know. We do feel, however, that we should make more of the superlative opportunity which the airplane affords, of recording the grandeur of the world. When we have looked entranced at some of those records made of cloud and serried summit as the airplane passed over them, we have felt that here, indeed, is a new avenue by which the appeals of nature may reach man. Vast, enthralling, awful, ecstatic in color and form, these natural glories unfold, heaven above heaven, until the beholder's mind is drenched in a succession of inspirations. The reaction is one which causes us to marvel at the capacities of our human nature for taking in the wonders of beauty. Formerly we saw the stars. Now we see the earth, the more beautiful and the more enticing vision. But we would not forget the stars. Having both these revelations, we have all.

Culture is a word fought over. It means to the reader whatever he takes in of impression, and whatever he creates out of it by contemplation. Certainly it is one of the grander hopes of our age that beauty and power may be so unrolled on human vision, and so correlated by human thought that the life of the twentieth-century man may mean much more than that of life in any other century. We seem to see a poet, a patriot, or an historian gliding with an enlightened imagination over the more splendid natural beauties. From Mount Desert to Moosehead Lake and the Appalachian chain; from Champlain to the Hudson, over the savannahs of New York and Pennsylvania, surveying the Water Gap and the sweeps of the Susquehanna, turning to the great architectural creations of our cities, to the banding railroads and the craft plying on the waters; and finally to the millions of dear and sweet abodes in suburb and country, — we may conceive of a large and noble intelligence suffused by these visions, made able to give us of human nature's best in poetry and art and patriotism. We love to dwell upon the reaction of man to the infinite phases of the world about him. The knowledge of chemistry, which is rising, — a miraculous body of facts gathered from liquid and gas and stone, from the mine and the air, is perhaps the most splendid exhibit of modern human achievement. Such a body of knowledge constantly growing, constantly wedded by and brooded over by the imagination, constantly applied and adapted to the uses and delights of man, suggests a very much larger human existence. This experience should make each individual life eventually mean a thousandfold as much as it does now.

We will say that a stolid laborer drives his spade full depth into mellow loam, and lifts it to gaze at it for a moment. What does it mean to him? Even to him it means much. But what does it mean to the chemist, what to the economist, what to the poet? In that spadeful is the beauty of all lilies and all roses. There are hid the hydrangea, the hyacinth, the

A WITCH FOOT BARN

iris. There are latent all the old-fashioned flowers. There are the grains
that nourish all men, with their simple, quiet, steady, gray white, innocu-
ous but delicious contents. There, also, are the secrets of geologic history.
The aeons are contained in every grain of earth. The flood has washed
it or the volcano has hurled it out. The sun has worked upon it its mystic
alchemy. It has transformed poisons. It has been the food of worms.
It is the source of the vegetable, the vegetable is the source of the animal,
the animal is the home or the companion or the cause of reaction, as we
choose to put it, of the spiritual. In that clod is history and science and
art and religion. We love a spadeful of soft, brown, fine earth. To sift
it in our fingers, to press it about a transplanted shoot, to smell its fragrant
power, to own it as a necessity, and to be given possession of it, to manipu-
late it, is, if we put our thought into it and derive its secrets from it, among
the best experiences of life.

If there is so much in a spadeful, what is there in a worldful? One
sweet, broad valley of Pennsylvania, prepared by nature and man, is suffi-

cient, under ideal conditions, under ideal stimulus of the mind and the heart, under proper adaptation of the economic and political sense, to provide a newer and a better Athens, a more permanently beautiful and inspiring Galilee, a steadier, a mightier and a more beneficent Rome.

It is not without a hint of the fine reaction upon the soul of nature that we find in Pennsylvania the names of Galilee and Ephrata the Fruitful, of Bethlehem and Bethany, of Hebron, Jordan, and Sharon. All these names are indubitable evidence that the heart of man moves upon the heart of nature. They prove that man, beginning again in a new world, dares to believe that it is worth while to raise up new ideals from the ruins of old ones. They show a beautiful and undying faith that the work of a thoughtful and diligent man on the soil of the earth, and that man's sweet and sane relations with his neighbors, are elements which may soon, and sometime must, evolve a satisfactory society. When we have wandered over such counties as Lancaster and Lebanon, Montgomery and Bucks, and have seen what man has done, how smoothly he has combed his fields, how neatly he has made his bounds, how carefully he has erected his habitations, we have been conscious of a kind of flood of gratitude, that men have achieved so much, and have spread themselves in a manner so wise and sane, over a tract of God's country. We cannot, however, resist the impression that this achievement is not enough, and that the men who labor here are not, or ought not to be, satisfied with what they have done. As yet their Bethlehem and Bethany lack particularly, we should say, most of all, that spirit which pushes on to acquire the crowning features of manhood. We hope for every farmer to feel the poetry that is in the sod. We hope for him to see the tawdriness in our churches under the so perfect sky. We feel as certain as we are of the sunrise that he will take as a recipe something of the soil, something of the rock, something of the cloud and the blue, something from the dreaming river, and by the alchemy of love and study and imagination and experience eventually produce works in literature and other lines of human achievement, for which the world is half famished. To us a landscape is not so much

BUCK HILL FALL

A RIVER IN HASTE—WINONA FALLS

A SHADOWED RIBBON ROAD—POCONO MOUNTAINS

POCONO BLOOMS

DOWN BY THE BARN—POCONO MOUNTAINS

PARADISE FALLS

ABANDONED IN THE CORN—BUCKS COUNTY

an achievement as a prophecy. The brooks tell of something that is coming, for which the past has been a long preparing foundation.

Two hundred years ago England was said to be over-populated when it had a small fraction of its present people in numbers. We heard the fatuity of Matthew Arnold state that England was finished. Well, it was nearly finished by the late war. It has been nearly finished by the disease and the blindness and the selfishness in it. It was nearly finished in the view of Goldsmith, when he wrote " The Deserted Village." England is an old country. Our known history is but a chapter to its overflowing volume. But who, noting the struggle upward in England at the present time, can doubt that the centuries have something vastly better for her than she has seen? Even from the standpoint of the physical, the useless lands of England are in time to be transformed. How much in the way of putting flowers in its alleys and sweet air where smoke reigns, how much in enriching the lives of the uneducated and improving for the multitude the possible harmonies that may be established between men as well as between men and nature, is yet to be done in England. If that is true in the Old World, what can we say of a fair region like Pennsylvania?

LANCASTER COUNTY

CARRYING forward a résumé of the attractions in this state, we find in this county a leadership claimed over all others in the Union. It is stated that the products of the soil in one year here have amounted to more than a hundred million dollars. We might traverse many prairie lands and search abroad in vain for fields as fair, as uniformly good, as well stocked, as well provided with storehouses and dwellings, as well fenced, as well kept. Nature was most fair and most rich. Man has been most diligent and intelligent in fostering and working with and on the earth. What an achievement to point out to the people of Russia! How long will it be before a similar area in Russia will exhibit a similar sanity, diligence, and wealth? Here is, perhaps, the banner district in the world of a similar area. It can teach the East and the West very much. To our southern compatriots, it may give a lesson well worth their conning, a lesson which it may require generations for them to learn and use.

Lancaster itself is of course a great market town, in the best old English sense, in many respects. It is also a teeming manufacturing center. It has its noble churches, the dean of which we presume is admitted to be St. Peter's (page 33), sketched for us by Mr. Carl W. Drepperd. In every direction from this well built city one goes inevitably to a premier agricultural district. If one wants to see what farming is, let him go to this county. The billowing grain in sea green, summer green, and August gold, rolls over the hills. The corn fields rustle and hide their full, silken ears, the finest aspect of any crop that grows. The orchards hang lusciously with all that succession of fruit which most aptly typifies the close of the year. Whether we see the close-set shocks of grain, or the abundant delicacies thriving in the garden, or the great, open doors of the barns that house all, there is driven in upon us that here is land doing its best, and men doing their best for it, and each enriched and made better by the result. Yet, as we have said, all this is only a preparation. Talk with any farmer or merchant and you find him to be full of information on certain subjects. He knows them about as well as they can be known. He has handled them, experimented with them, and called in sun, rain, and chemicals to win success by them. He knows his work and rests in quiet assurance regarding it. Touch him on those aspects of his life to which he has principally given his attention, and you derive a full and satisfactory reaction. But there are lines of thought, profitable for him to follow, upon which neither he nor we have gone very far. There is an unrealized world for every man. Neither need he go to heaven to find it. It is above the mines and below the stars. His feet stand upon it, and his hands have to do with it. But let no farmer, let no mechanic, think that he has done more than touch the surface of things.

A BARN NEAR ALLENTOWN

As a man with a small vocabulary wrestles with the expression of a few crude thoughts, and regards with dull astonishment the plethoric torrent of Shakespeare's ideas, so any mechanic or farmer, or scholar, when he thinks, knows full well that he is working around the edges or upon certain facets of his subject. What a broader education and the light of imagination, and the careful setting to work of chemical discovery, can make of men and their surroundings, is an unsolved, a fascinating problem. What an intelligent Pennsylvania farmer is in comparison with an Egyptian laborer is the distance of centuries of experience, a zone of climate, the prayers, the struggles, the genius of ages. What the Pennsylvania farmer is to the man who will work upon the same soil a thousand years from now, we do not at all know. But we feel compelled, by the forces of an undiscouraged evolution around us eternally at work, to conclude that some time, on this soil, there will break forth a finer quality of civilization than America now possesses.

The initial and perhaps fatal historic mistake of human thought is that it has arbitrarily divided itself into categories, and has gratuitously assumed a lack of unity between the component parts of creation. Just as if the sod could be separated from the stars, just as if argon and hydrogen were not as divine in their intended uses as hymns. Who, in these days, is big enough or wise enough or bold enough to separate the agencies in nature from what we have been accustomed to call spirit? Who in the re-arrangement of knowledge would be so fatuous as to keep chemistry out of religion, or religion out of chemistry? Who knows that there is not as much moral purpose in a sunbeam as in a commandment?

A little south of Lancaster the Conestoga river and the Little Conestoga form beautiful dells, and one of the loveliest river bank strolls that we have found in the state. There is literally a picture at every turn, by which we mean a really artistic composition.

Pequa Creek, a little south of the Conestoga, is another pictorial stream. We came hereabouts, near Quarryville, upon a row of fruit trees in blossom and overhanging a little field canal. It is one of the finest instances of the fact that intimate subjects in the immediate foreground afford the greatest satisfaction (page 79).

Anent the Conestoga, the name is freighted with romance, since it was from this locality that the Conestoga wagon took its name. This remarkable craft, if one may use the term as we are tempted to do by the boat shape of the body, is the finest symbolical embodiment of western emigration. The vehicle was wide and high and long, equipped with axe, bucket, and every possible appliance for restoring the ravages of fire and freshet, to make a mountain road passable again. The shape of the bottom of the vehicle was adopted in order to prevent the shifting of the load on steep hills. This vehicle was of the type regularly in use for the great emigration and great freight movement that followed it into the states of Ohio, Kentucky, and beyond. The ordinary prairie schooner was a poor country cousin of the Conestoga wagon. One of these vehicles ought to be kept in the museum of every great city in the regions settled through their use, that the generations may see how their fathers crossed the mountain and the flood.

WATER BOWS—POCONO MOUNTAINS

A POCONO HOME DRIVE

APPLE COTTAGE—NEAR STROUDSBURG

A WEST CHESTER BORDER

BRIDE'S WAY—POCONO MOUNTAINS

OLD TIME PENNSYLVANIA—LANCASTER COUNTY

THE LEHIGH AT PLAY—LUZERNE COUNTY

SHADOW DELL—LUZERNE COUNTY

A POCONO POOL

A SCRANTON STREAM

A PENNSYLVANIA BORDER

A DOUBLE LEAP—POCONO MOUNTAINS

UPPER LADDER FALLS—POCONO MOUNTAINS

A LINCOLN ROADSIDE—WEST CHESTER COUNTY

We reserve for future treatment the Susquehanna border of Lancaster County, as well as of those counties that lie to the northwest of it and on the east of the great river.

BERKS COUNTY

THE city of Reading, the centre of this teeming county, is thoroughly well built, but for the most part lies outside the scope of our work. Its Trinity Lutheran church-spire (page 33) is one of the most beautiful in Pennsylvania, being quite different in type from those of New England, yet with special merits of its own. One of these is that it was constructed of permanent materials, as those in New England for the most part are not. It presides over the centre of the city in a very comforting manner. As one enters the town, an edifice with much the appearance of a European castle or a great armory, we are told, is the jail. Before it, a great pear tree was in beautiful blossom (page 152).

Four or five miles east of Reading the stream which meanders through the golf course calls out our admiration (page 15). Another stream to the south of the road beneath the elms and the buttonwoods, and called the Monocacy, offers the best pictorial opportunities which we discovered in the county (page 12). We love best these streams with gently sloping banks, but with just enough good nature to turn the wheels of the little old mills. Berks County has extensive highlands to the east and north of Reading, and somewhat high land to the south. These hills are detached from the main chain of the Appalachians, and enjoy an individuality and beauty of their own. Moving easterly, near Boyertown, we find ourselves in a rich agricultural valley settled by the Germans, and with many quaint architectural features. The ancient customs are largely handed down, with little change. The entire drive from Reading through Boyertown and thence northeast to Allentown, or bearing still more east through Quakertown and toward Bethlehem, is less marked by open plains than we find to be the rule in Lancaster County. But the gentle hills and the numerous turns give the country an older, cosier, more pleasing effect pictorially.

MONTGOMERY COUNTY

NORRISTOWN, itself rather notable for early homes and collections of earlier furniture, is also a convenient region for exploring Montgomery County. The streams of this county excel, for our purposes, any others we have seen in the state. The Perkiomen river, having its sources in Berks, Lehigh, and Bucks, meanders through the county in many a delightful curve. It has furnished us (pages 25, 26, 36, 46, 50, 67, 68) with numerous records of its beauties. There are stately arches seeming to exist purely to tempt the wanderer to make a sylvan camp on the banks. There is many an old flour mill, some of them still active. One could pass an entire week with delight canoeing on this stream.

The Skippack, quite near to Norristown, is only second in attraction to the Perkiomen. This stream invites us to be children again, and to wade in its sands and play with its pebbles. A lunch on its grassy banks, beneath the broad leaves of the buttonwoods, is an experience that may sweeten several stormy winter days, as we recall, by our firesides, the shimmering reaches of the Skippack.

At Collegeville, the main western highway, about seven miles from Norristown, crosses a bridge said to have been built about 1800. Its fine ramps and the little bastions over the piers, — an ideal spot for the fisherman, the artist, the poet, or the lover, — the quiet waters beneath, their banks lined with noble trees, may continue to hold us in longing admiration. There is an ancient tavern at one end of the bridge, and the town, with its educational flavor, spreads fair beyond on the higher slopes.

Northeast from Ambler, which in contiguous to Norristown, one drives through a semi-urban neighborhood. The place names add not a little to the flavor of such a tour. One passes, for instance, through Plymouth

THE MORAVIAN CHURCH — BETHLEHEM

Meeting. On the other side of the Schuylkill is the village called "King of Prussia." When names are so easy of access, we never fail to wish that these romantic terms are not more in use.

Norristown is the natural point from which Valley Forge is reached, though if one comes from Philadelphia and keeps to the south of the Schuylkill he follows another interesting route, on which we found "The Curving Lane" (page 47), that fed our feeling for a gently sloping countryside. It was on this journey, also, near Phoenixville, that we found the farm whose dwelling is shown (page 23) in "A Pennsylvania Cottage." The apple tree at the back door is the one thing we should always insist on. There ought to be a law that no detached dwelling should be without an apple tree. Is it not a law of sentiment, of convenience, and of social harmony and unity? Will it not keep the children at home and bring them back after they are grown? The dear lady who is housewife in this dwelling came out and picked us flowers, and rejoiced in our joy over her home. Persons owning dwellings like these are more outside of them than inside. From a distance, on the opposite side, this place is seen again (page 48) in the picture entitled " The Creek in May." Multitudes of white flowers grew in front of the dwelling on the bank of the stream. This spot was a haven of peace and kindly comfort and homely joys.

Valley Forge has now happily been redeemed to form a shrine of the American people. We secured a composition which connects the stream with the headquarters in our picture on page 57. The house in which Washington lived here is small. It is opened widely to the public, and supplies a kind of educational centre in patriotism, and gives a glimpse of the old manner of living. Particularly interesting is the kitchen end. In Pennsylvania the log kitchen is not so very rare, though we have never seen one retained in the east and north. A peculiar feature of many stone farm houses is the placing of the chimney at the outside angle of the ell, so that it comes up from a corner, a fashion we have not seen elsewhere in America. Within, this corner was occupied by a vast platform for doing all the baking and boiling of the household, together with the larger operations, such as the autumn killing. Beneath this great platform the flues ran from more than one direction toward the chimney. The floor was flagged. The room was large, and hung about with great ladles, skillets, broilers, and griddles. It would require indeed a page to catalog all the characteristic utensils ranged around the two interior walls. A room like this, while not especially pictorial, engages one's absorbed attention. It was for a considerable part of the day the home of the housewife, though originally we understand its use was confined mostly to the warmer season of the year.

LAFAYETTE'S HEADQUARTERS—WEST CHESTER COUNTY

A PENNSYLVANIA COTTAGE—NEAR POTTSVILLE

MOUNTAIN WEALTH—IN THE POCONOS

INDEPENDENCE HALL

LUZERNE WATERS

DELAWARE CANAL AT EASTON

RIVER FOG

APPLE TREE WAY

A Pennsylvania farmer's wife is the most efficient person imaginable. She is not thin and nervous, as New England women sometimes were. She is the image of large contentment. Her heart is in her work. It is not a means with her, but an end. She seems sorry that her baking should ever be done, but if by any chance she can think of nothing more to do in the outer kitchen, she turns to the embroidery of linen, toweling, or to the making of some design in a bedspread. From age to age every house-wife desires to add a little touch of originality to the conventions of the days that were. Her chests of drawers, of fine old walnut, groan with their burden of counterpanes and linen sheets. Her samplers adorn the walls and her rugs cover the floors.

There is no form of farm labor that belongs to woman which this woman cannot do in perfection, and which she does not love. The cheese and the butter-making, the sauerkraut and the apple-butter put up in vast quantities in the autumn, the preserves and dried fruit and vegetables, would fill no mean storehouse for a garrison. These people labor largely, and a Pennsylvania farmer's appetite is in proportion to his size and his efforts. Dyspepsia is not a chronic ailment. The corned beef and the mincemeat, the ham and the bacon, and the host of other substantial or more dainty stores, fill the great cellars. Any farmer seeking a wife should haunt the rural districts of Pennsylvania, where women were born to be farmers' wives, and where they continually thank God for the fact! They justly believe there is no higher estate. Ample in dimensions physically, serene of mind, endowed with broad common sense, loving her home and her acres, the Pennsylvania farmer's wife is a true helpmeet for her husband.

The spirit so common in other parts of our country where the farm is thought the plaything for rich retired persons, or a half-despised way station for those who aspire to a trade or profession, is happily wanting on the typical Pennsylvania farm. While we would not say that every man ought to be content where he is and with what he is doing, we can but feel that there must be for the permanence of our institutions a great many such persons as are found in rural Pennsylvania.

Those who meander through our picture pages will find other examples belonging to this county.

CHESTER COUNTY

LET us say at once, to avoid the wrath of our numerous friends in West Chester, that all the pictures in this volume which are both titled and placed as in Chester, refer to Chester County, and not to Old Chester, with the exception of those that are specially so designated.

Old Chester, from its location near the river Delaware, and from its proximity to large manufacturing enterprises and its more level contours, has not supplied us with so much pictorial material as has Chester County. Indeed, Chester is in Delaware County.

West Chester believes itself to be the finest type of a suburban town, and there is very much in it and about it to justify the belief. It has attractive public buildings and ancient inns, with a prestige and a romance worthy of the pen of Dickens or Thackeray. Its private residences possess much dignity and charm, particularly that which is derived from eighteenth-century architecture and decorations. Old trees, old shrubs, old walks, old cornices, old fireplaces and furniture, old customs and old friendships are other names for West Chester.

Large schools here add an agreeable scholastic flavor. The region round about is sought out by those who, having attained a competence and a knowledge of the world, desire to plant themselves for generations, for they think of their children as reincarnations. When we asked about a certain resident, we were informed that he was not known very well, because he had been there only forty years! People who write and think, and other people who perhaps just sit, as they say in the South, have flocked to the districts bordering West Chester. All this is very alluring

THE CLOISTERS, EPHRATA

to one with the writer's cast of mind, who can think of no region more agreeable to live in or to die in. It is thoroughly adapted either for thinking or for sitting.

But let not the frivolous imagine that West Chester does not know itself, or that it is narrow. Let anybody come along who is worth while and is also a gentleman, and he will be adopted into the families of West Chester with as much cordiality as if he had been there longer.

We have found the environment of West Chester just what we love. The first immediate object of delight is the Brandywine at Chad's Ford, that wonderful old bridge which, with its neighborhood, shows in different aspects on pages 45 and 67. The picture of cows shows them interested but contented in the buttonwood meadows below the bridge. The site is that of the Battle of Brandywine, and Lafayette's Headquarters appear on page 119. The Brandywine and its tributaries are hereabouts all that we can ask in the way of beauty. "A West Chester Border," page 119, gives us an orchard enclosed by a zigzag rail fence. "A Lincoln Roadside" is close to the college, some miles west of West Chester. The region is rich in little valley nooks, like "A Dogwood Bank" and "Blossom Valley" on page 145. "The Bride's Shower," page 151, where, in spite of the innumerable petals on the ground, there seem to be innumerable others above, is found in the same region, as are the pictures on page 153, one on page 163, and "The Guarded Home" on page 165. The clouds favored us in "A Chester Valley," page 117, and bridge and stream and road and tree in "A Mill and a Dell," page 183. "Penn's Woods," page 184, "A Petaled Cart Path," page 203, and particularly "A Blossoming Arch," page 215, delighted us. The proximity of West Chester to Philadelphia has made it feasible for many to take advantage of its loveliness. The neighborhood appears more thoroughly English than any other section of America with which we are familiar.

We have mentioned the inns of West Chester. We should further say that not only in the town, but on many roads leading from it we have the characteristic stone-built, old-fashioned inns, where it is still possible to obtain a substantial meal. Everything is placed on the table. We counted thirteen kinds of vegetables and sauces on the occasion of finding ourselves at such an inn. The walls were thick and the windows were splayed in the English stone farm house fashion, so that even on the interior these old dwellings give the feeling of security and permanence. We do not expect the walls of inns to be adorned with works of art. A curious cupboard of walnut is all that we can ask. Nor do we ask in vain.

The Pennsylvania inn seems to be able to continue in a fashion under the eighteenth amendment. Perhaps the milder beverages are not so satisfactory to the old customer, but they will answer for us boys. Some of the old inns have gathered curious old implements or furniture, which they have attached to the ceiling or otherwise disposed about the rooms, so as to prove an attraction to the mind. If prohibition has done this, we thank it. It is a higher appeal, and in the end may prove just as expensive to the customer and as profitable to the inn-keeper!

It is hard for us to tear ourselves away from West Chester, and we find our feet, or should we say our steering-gear, inclined to turn that way. For beauty, for physical improvements, for architectural dignity, for quiet and good society, for an educational atmosphere, and for convenience to great centres, we have loved the town.

OLD CHESTER COURT HOUSE

THE WASHINGTON CHURCH AT VALLEY FORGE

IT has required an unique combination of talents to erect a church of a memorial nature like that at Valley Forge. The result is monumental, and the labor required is no less than colossal. The devoted man who here exercises his functions as a clergyman has given many years with his artistic advisers to the production of an edifice, in every stone and timber of which there is the feeling of ancient memories. The windows are commemorative of notable events and persons of the Revolution. Even the carvings in the choir stalls and other features of the edifice are especially designed to the same end. For a unified work it speaks at once of reverence, knowledge, patience, and good taste. There is scarcely anything in America that is comparable with this edifice and its contents. Our picture, page 229, shows it in the spring, when only its outlines are visible through the limbs of the trees. An open cloister is well begun, each section of which is being undertaken by different parts of the Union. Long may the noble and sincere soul who has done this service to his country continue, so that if possible in his lifetime he may see a certain degree of completion. In the basement, perhaps we should say crypt, he has gathered also an immense number of articles in use during the ancient time, and characteristic mostly of Pennsylvania. They include not only such things as are usually found in museums, but many of a peculiarly valuable character connected with the personalities or the spirit of patriotism of the past.

Of course, in process of time it is the purpose to erect a separate museum for the important collection. The spirit of pure unselfishness which has been manifested in this labor should certainly stimulate us all to assist in its purpose.

A MONTGOMERY COUNTY HOMESTEAD

BUCKS COUNTY

AS old, as finished, as pleasing as any of the counties in the state, Bucks, just north of Philadelphia, and on the route of all those who go to the Water Gap, to the Poconos, or to the north, demands a good deal of the traveler's attention if he would get the spirit of Pennsylvania.

At Doylestown, Dr. Mercer, the author of *The Bible in Iron*, has erected a monumentally solid fireproof museum to show the connection between the development of household arts and the invention of tools and implements. Dr. Mercer has given most generously of his years and otherwise to this great, and in many respects unique institution. It is his right, and perhaps his purpose, to deal with his collections in a scientific and literary manner, in order that the public may everywhere enjoy the fruits of his labors and studies. There are other collections in the neighborhood which, however, are not open to public use. In this neighborhood a careful study is being made by various persons, under the inspiration of Dr. Mercer, of the earliest Pennsylvania institutions, such as its forges, foundries, and ancient industries. Also the peculiar styles of architecture in this state are being carefully studied, and various persons have erected or restored dwellings in the best early taste. In fact, all about Philadelphia there has been a rather successful effort to idealize country life. The thoughts of the founders have been carried out as they would like to have carried them out had they possessed the leisure or the means. In an effort of this sort there has been too often, in other parts of the country, a grafting on of modern or individual notions to such an extent as to ruin the unity of development. About Philadelphia we find a more careful attention to bring things back as they were, or as the fathers meant to make them. Even when, as very often occurs, wealth, and a desire to entertain largely induces the erection of a dwelling larger than a farm house, the work is often as if it were an extension of such a farm house. To our thought this is the only proper course. Mixing the old and the new spoils each. The more rigorous, the more thoroughly correct we are, the greater the charm, and the more meritorious will be the result.

In the dwelling itself, therefore, the spirit of the Pennsylvania home should first be conserved in the solidness of the stone wall, and in the use of flagging or brick in such rooms as the kitchen, the den, or any large home room where such construction would be historically proper. The heavy window frames should be insisted upon, and the deep embrasures of the splayed windows. Large fireplaces, open to their full extent and to some degree in use, must certainly form a part of the scheme. We were told recently of the purchase of a so-called colonial house which had no fireplaces whatever. Of course the house was either very much after the colonial time, or its fireplaces had been completely built up and hidden, the more likely alternative. No bricks should ever be used where stone ever was used, or could be used.

[*Text continued on page 136.*]

SKIPPACK ELMS

A FRIENDLY BROOK

SHADOWS OF BUTTONWOODS—WEST CHESTER

ACCOMMODATING CURVES—WEST CHESTER

ALL FAIR IN MAY—ZIONSVILLE

A TUMULT OF WATERS—PARADISE VALLEY

THE OLD DRIVE

Written by MILDRED HOBBS for picture on page 133

Into a wonder-road the old drive led,
A road that beckoned youth to follow far,
So bright the vision, and the goal so great.
But when the race was won and time had sped
The road led homeward to the open gate.
And now to be returning
After the years of yearning!
The singing wheels, the sharp familiar turn,
Leaving behind the road of dreams-afar,
The boughs caressing as they did of yore,
The quickened pulse, the unshed tears that burn
At sight of Mother waiting at the door
Where lilacs stoop to kiss her silvering hair
And wave to us across the scented air.

And so the long procession of the years —
The little children swinging on the gate,
The sweethearts strolling on the moonlit grass
Beneath the trees who shed their petal-tears
For phantom friends as up and down they pass
With dreams of restless roaming
Or songs of homing.
A long procession up and down the drive —
The relatives and neighbors congregate
For wedding feasts and times of death and birth,
And dear-loved faces of the past arrive,
The old drive, silent, sad, or loud with mirth.
Oh, what a wealth of memories endears
These petal-covered curves, deep-scarred with years!

The ceilings of the type found in the middle Atlantic states in the early period are beautifully appropriate. They were in the form of thin, but deep floor timbers, which were smoothly dressed by plane, as well as the floors that were laid above them. The open ceiling of a New England house was of necessity somewhat crude, as the summer beam was often the only smooth portion. If the smaller floor timbers were smooth, the floor above never was. In the Brown house, already referred to, a perfectly clean ceiling is obtained. Sometimes the work seems to have been done in walnut, and sometimes in poplar or whitewood. We presume pine was used on occasion, though it seems to have been rather rare. Ceilings of this sort are seen in old-world houses, though we have never seen here the corbels which are found abroad at the end of the floor timbers. The nearest approach to these corbels is the enlarged, splayed post familiar in seventeenth-century New England houses. We refer to a corbel somewhat like the bracket previously mentioned as sustaining the door head on the Black Horse Tavern.

The construction with long deep timbers, entirely spanning a room, was stronger than the summer beam type, and was less likely to sag in the middle.

The habit of building in long cupboards in wood, in Pennsylvania, was a very practical device. We find it some times in long hallways. The cupboard thus formed a finish of the wall on the side of the room where it was located, for it extended the entire width and obviated an unpleasant break.

We notice that the fireplaces in Pennsylvania were often open to a greater height than those found farther north. This also is a more faithful following of the tradition of the Old World. Some of the trammels which we possess could not have been used except in a very high fireplace, since they must have hung at least nine feet above the floor. One should remember that at first there was no crane.

The treatment of the wall ought also, of course, to be in wood for partitions, and where feasible, even for the outer walls of stone a cover-

A PHILADELPHIA HOMESTEAD

ing of the simplest panel work could be provided. The styles of molding about the doors and on the doors themselves could be followed, except where, as in the quainter examples, solid doors were used. The stairway in Pennsylvania was not made as much of as commonly in New England, but wherever the genius of the locality will permit, it should be emphasized in its quainter or more beautiful aspects. Externally the water tables should be used, as in " The Ancient Abandoned Farm House," page 102. In a large dwelling this water table can be repeated between the first and second stories, as in examples already mentioned. As to the roof, we may be told that it was necessary to use shingles to keep the old feeling. But in a country so full of slate that even the fence posts are often of that material, it is obvious that a heavy slate, with roughly chipped edges, like the English Horsham slate, may be used, and thus make for fire protection. No dwelling of this sort is completely happy without flags at the back door and flag paths elsewhere, wherever the extent of the grounds or the means of the builder will permit. We have long felt the appropriateness of the name " flag " for these flat stones, which in England were often laid across marshes where the flags grew, or were placed upon the floor and were covered over with flags from the marshes. We have sought in vain, however, to find some connection between the name of the stone and the growing flag.

It often happens that an old house is restored or a new one built in the old style without taking account of some of the best features of the old time. Thus the sentiment and the connection are lost, and a great part of the effort is in vain. The furniture, for instance, should agree quite perfectly with the type and the period of the house. Let no one think to toss this matter lightly aside by stating that there is no effort to have the furniture in period. That is generally obvious enough, in fact too much so, without making such a statement. But it is not enough to deny an intention where an intention ought to have existed; nor is it enough to answer that people may follow their own tastes. That also is too obvious, but it does not establish their social or aesthetic right to do so. When it

WATER STAIRS—POCONO

SPRING TURBULENCE—POCONO

PINE FALLS—POCONO

A SCRANTON CASCADE

WATER PLAY—POCONO

THE JOY OF THE YEAR—MONROE

SPRING BROOK ROAD

AN UNNAMED CASCADE—POCONO

SPRING DELL——CHESTER

A HOME IN SPRINGTIME——LANCASTER

BY THE FENCE

LIGHTS OF THE RIVER

A WEST CHESTER BLOSSOM VALLEY

DOGWOOD BANKS—CHESTER

A CROWDED BROOK—DELAWARE WATER GAP

MOUNTAIN BORN—POCONO

is a fad to take up early architecture and decoration, those who are merely following fads always make the mistake of lacking thoroughness. The result is somewhat like that obtained in Japan and China, by the adoption of occidental costumes, on the part of women, who then dress the hair in the oriental style. Many an American lady, who would be shocked if every portion of her costume was not in perfect accord, in style and color, with every other portion, does not hesitate to throw together a tasteless jumble in her residence. It is like the nabobs of India bringing in a few occidental pieces of furniture. Particularly in the decorative arts, one should do all or none. A thing of this sort, half done, has an effect far worse than an original condition, however bad.

It is true that there is no modern furniture, in the sense that any style has established itself, or is likely to do so. We have had neither the time nor the segregation, nor the art impulse, nor anything else, perhaps, required to originate a harmonious and sensible style of household decoration. So many good men have preceded us, and have thought of so much that is good, that we are handicapped. We are also hindered by the lack of that seclusion which an artist requires in order to specialize. Perhaps we are naturally inartistic. Whatever the cause for present conditions, it is far safer to copy than to originate. It is less necessary, perhaps, to say these things in a book on Pennsylvania than it would be to say them in a book on the West. Yet these principles would not come amiss anywhere, and cannot be too often reiterated. It will be time enough to stop enunciating them when they begin to be heeded. There is a very powerful sentimental impulse to keep what our mothers had. But if those mothers, or their mothers, did not feel that impulse in sufficient strength to keep what *their* mothers had, then we would do best to hark back to the great grandmothers, where at last we shall arrive at some dignity and harmony and sense in style.

It is a good place here to point out some of the features in furnishings which were distinctive in the middle Atlantic states, and which usually go by the name " Pennsylvanian."

The settle, with a paneled back and often with a hooded top, and with a fine ramp on the arm, is more frequently found in Pennsylvania than elsewhere. We have observed there also several instances of settle beds, two of them being in beautifully finished walnut. The seat swings outward and downward. Near the bottom thus disclosed there are bed rails which are made a part of the piece of furniture, and sustain a corded bed close to the floor. The rails are cut in two at the ends in order to fold with the seat. This is a very curious and important article in furniture. It is one more evidence that the devices which we call modern were useful in an early day, and in a form perhaps superior to our own.

The cupboards found in Pennsylvania are interesting in their scalloped cornices, the scallop being under the molding and forming the upper part of the opening to the top shelf. The scrolled edge comes forward rapidly at the bottom of the side member which sustains the shelves, and forms a sort of foot to hold the upper section of the cupboard on the dresser. In the good specimens, the molding is of the eighteenth-century type. There is often a light rail between the shelves to prevent the dishes from falling forward. There is generally a series of slots on one shelf for a row of spoons. For illustrations, the reader is referred to the author's *Furniture of the Pilgrim Century*. A variation of these cupboards was a smaller form suspended on the wall, with similar scrolls. It often accompanied a cupboard of similar width, placed on the floor below, and with the top arranged for a wash-stand or a mixing bowl. The corner cupboards, with handsomely paneled doors, existed in great numbers. In fact, a good Pennsylvania house was supplied with such a great number and variety of cupboards as to make them an impressive feature. No doubt this peculiarity arose from the heavy stone construction of the house walls. A northern house would have had its cupboard built in, with doors matching the other doors of the dwelling, and with lath and plaster. We feel that the Pennsylvanian type was far superior.

The cradles in use in Pennsylvania were often attractively scrolled, and with the hand hold in the shape of a heart or a shield at either end, and

FRIENDS' MEETING HOUSE, BUCKINGHAM

with a series of knobs on the outside, near the top, to which was buttoned the coverlet.

The distinctive chair of Pennsylvania is the arched slat back, rising in the better instances to six, and, in rare examples, to seven slats. The chair is one of the most striking and attractive ever made. Furthermore, it is very comfortable. It was, in the original state, made with enlarged balls upon the front feet, though these have for the most part been sawed off.

The tables sometimes belong to the library and at other times to the kitchen, with a large one piece top, and something like two by four feet in dimensions, often had an attractively scalloped frame, and were of heavy turning with stretchers. The knobs were always very large on the drawers, of which there were generally two or three of unequal length.

The chests of Pennsylvania (page 287) were in the finest examples of walnut. We find them also in pine and poplar, but never, so far as we have observed, in oak. The feet ordinarily were in the form of brackets, and the better examples were paneled and often had inlaid initials. Some very handsome designs, together with others less handsome, were painted on chests. The tulip design predominates, the motive being either Dutch or derived from the Dutch by the Germans. So persistent has style and custom been in Pennsylvania that these chests, found as early as 1700, are also observed in nearly the same style as late as the Civil War.

The walnut highboys of a plain kind are also characteristic of this state. The more ornate pieces of Savery and in the style of Savery are very much enriched by carving, and have bonnet tops with a cartouche and flames. These pieces, of course, belong to the richer houses, and the mahogany period, though walnut was used to a very late date on fine furniture in Pennsylvania.

The wall decorations, aside from the conventional paintings, such as would be purchased by persons of wealth and taste, were samplers or old prints.

We have not observed in the Pennsylvania Museum that much atten-

A BRIDE'S SHOWER

THE BROOK ROW—CHESTER

CREST BLOSSOMS—CHESTER

A BRANDYWINE CROSSING—CHESTER

THE HOME STRETCH—NEAR READING

tion has yet has been paid to the characteristic pieces of Pennsylvania, especially the chests. No doubt this will be remedied in time.

It will be understood from the previous review that there was more harmony between the furniture and the wall in Pennsylvania than in northern dwellings. The color of the furniture and the wall blended happily.

Out of doors, the shingles or the slate were almost harmonious with the stone in many cases, or were in agreeable shadings suggesting the same color scheme.

The glassware made so famous by Stiegel and other makers is now sought after with the greatest avidity, so that little pieces which were probably sold for a few cents are now held at many hundreds of dollars. Of course a Pennsylvania home which retains, or can retrieve a few of these pieces, feels itself especially fortunate, and glass of course puts the last touches to the decorations of a home.

The slip ware, so common in Pennsylvania generations go, and so generally used, is quite ordinary pottery except for the strong local flavor imparted by the decorations. These are of the quaintest character, especially the inscriptions. Shiny limousines may be seen here and there on the remote hill roads. Their owners are engaged in a thrilling, though often futile, effort at bargaining for some of the old slip ware. In the hill homes, however, where the traditions of family and the pride of architecture do not so often exist, it is often possible to effect an exchange satisfactory to both parties. The slip ware is now counterfeited.

It occurs to us that several utensils used in Pennsylvania may, with interest, be mentioned. One is the large splayed bread tray with four splayed legs, a sharply localized institution. It indicated a large family and a wholesale baking. The water bench is another strictly local affair. It was a low shelf, often with cupboards below, and a board running up at each side in a scroll form, with a shelf above, and a drawer, the front of which, in some instances, is made on a curve corresponding with the scroll. These benches were long enough for two farm hands to lave themselves side by side. The drawer could be used for towels, one shelf for the basins and one shelf for the pails.

The Windsor chair, which also seems to have originated in Pennsylvania, so far as America is concerned, and to have remained there in its quainter and heavier forms, is now becoming rare and an object of worth and desire.

The utensils of iron within and without a Pennsylvania home were legion. In "An Ancient Kitchen," page 70, is shown a West Chester fireplace, though unfortunately a small one. The more interesting features are the small portable charcoal stove, the trivets, the toasters, the suspended griddle, and the pewter. The bellows are seen hanging at the left, together with an adjustable ceiling light. Of course the firearms were always kept over the fireplace to keep the power dry. The fat lamp, called in New England a Betty lamp, immediately over the gun stock, was very much used in Pennsylvania. In the better forms it was made double, as here, so that the lower portion might catch the drip. This picture shows, on the left, one of the six-back chairs so attractively arched, to which we have already referred. We show in the later pages of this volume the end of a loom-stool (page 285) owned by Mr. William B. Montague of Norristown. It is attractively painted in a tulip design, and there is a stanza in German below the slits. The loom-stool was not found in New England so far as we know, but only a board which must be held between the knees or tied to a chair. In the loom-stool, so called, one end held the board here shown, and near the other end was a small windlass reel. These looms were used for weaving narrow goods, like tape and garters, and were sometimes called garter looms. They should not be confused with the huge affairs on which yard-wide goods were woven.

An oddity peculiar to this region is also the buttonhole cutter (page 245), a four-rayed example of which we show. The points of different widths were used to cut buttonholes of the sizes desired, by striking a hammer on the tool applied to the goods laid on a cutting board. The

AN ARTIST'S NOOK, NEAR NEW HOPE

pointed ray or spoke was used for making eyelets for embroidery. The hammers also formed part of the buttonhole set, and were often wrought in quaint forms and used as gift pieces to sweethearts. This example is unique so far as we know, with the various spokes, each twisted.

Another peculiarity was the double ended utensil with a fork and a cake turner (page 244). Our example shows the open heart in the shovel end. Sets of four or five pieces consisting of fork, flapjack turner, ladle and skimmer, were common. They were all hand-hammered, of soft gray iron. Occasionally, however, the bowl is in hammered copper. In the handle, in rare examples, as Mr. William B. Montague's set, initials were inlaid in brass.

The rolling pin, of the better type, had a double roll and a handle above, and was of walnut, decorated. It would stand alone. The long wooden ladle for the apple-butter was another picturesque utensil. In another volume we have shown at length the various applied hardware of a Pennsylvania dwelling. We take this occasion to refer to some of the quaint iron work used out of doors.

The pump spout was sometimes supported by twisted and scrolled iron brackets. The immensely long and picturesque sickles for the grain were used up to a recent time. The goose and pig and calf yokes are most homelike in their appeal. Quaint hay cutters, pig catchers and short scythes help to form the complement of the farm tools.

The wagon work in Pennsylvania was as characteristic and substantial as the other domestic manufactures. The sides of the wagons were often paneled. In the northern part of the state the wagon seat now used as a small settle was somewhat in evidence, though this quaint affair is commoner in New York state. It is erroneously called a love seat, though no doubt many a young man and maid have found it, as they journeyed to town, a kind of courting seat.

The time was marked, in the ancient day, by sun dials and sand glasses, though the stomach was often a sufficiently sure indicator of the noon hour, so much so, indeed, that one farmer used to say that he could tell

THE RIVER BANK, HONESDALE

the time by his stomach within five minutes of correctness. So much for the regular habits of the Pennsylvanian!

We show one or two examples of the remarkably good combination locks and latches of iron, which we have found in Pennsylvania (page 277 and page 193). The more elaborate of these somewhat resembles the still finer sort found in the Old World, especially German examples, from the region whence the Pennsylvania settlers came. The oddest feature about these latches is that the exterior handle was in the nature of a somewhat cumbrous scroll, and was attached by a very short screw thread. When the family went to market or retired for the night, this was unscrewed and it was a notice to the public that privacy was desired. It answered the same purpose as the pulling in of the latch string in the cruder and earlier day. The appliance would be awkward in a modern pocket, but in the old days the larger this screw handle was, the less likely was it to be lost. Perhaps after the Saturday's visitation to the inn, it was convenient to have a key that would jump up into one's hand!

We cannot leave this subject without noting a feature of decoration which has long delighted the writer, namely the carved or painted spoon rack, on which were displayed, in two of three rows, a dozen pewter spoons brilliant with polishing, while at the base of the contrivance there was often a drawer in which the knives and forks were stored (pages 257 and 265). All these racks seem to show a Dutch influence, and indeed we are able to trace the style to a particular province in Holland — Friesland. They are therefore more common in New Jersey than in Pennsylvania, but one or two of these examples were found in the latter state. No more pleasing wall ornament could be devised for a living room. That always desirable feature, the combination of decoration and use in one article is found in the spoon rack.

There are instances in Pennsylvania where the entire wall is decorated with stencils or scrolls on the plaster.

LOOKING GLASSES

THE Pennsylvania Museum, in a recent bulletin, has shown a score or so of interesting labels found on the backs of looking glasses made by John Elliott. He was born at Bolton, England, in 1713, emigrated to America in 1753, and died in 1791. His name and that of his son of the same name, and those of his grandsons John and Daniel, are affixed on the backs of many Pennsylvania looking glasses. Most of the advertisements show a bell and a looking glass, below which there is descriptive text. The advertisements cover the years 1758–1759, in the article referred to. One in the *Pennsylvania Journal*, March 23, 1758, is as follows:

TALKING WATER. *By Sladen after Nutting*

Juſt imported from London, and to be ſold by
JOHN ELLIOT,
At his looking-glaſs ſtore, the ſign of the Bell and looking-glaſs
in Cheſtnut Street Philadelphia.
A neat aſſortment of looking-glaſſes: viz., Piers, ſconces, dreſſ-
ing- glaſſes, ſwingers, pocket glaſſes, ink and ſand bottles with
braſs covers. He alſo new quickſilvers and frames old glaſſes,
and ſupplies people with new glaſs to their frames.

The inference from this advertisement is that at this late date looking glasses were still for the most part imported. As we see, however, that Elliott quicksilvered old glasses and did general repairing, we may believe that the country was edging toward the manufacture of the glass. The time coincides with glass making in Pennsylvania, but we doubt if the superior quality of plate was produced until many years later. In one of the other advertisements an offer to make frames was recorded. The swinging glasses of course referred to the glass set upon a dressing table for the use of a lady, or as a shaving glass.

Elliott's use of the bell in his sign indicated that he also provided door and call bells for dwellings.

IN AND AROUND PHILADELPHIA

SUCH a multitude of books showing houses of the late colonial period have shown the dwellings of Germantown and the other well known houses of Philadelphia, that we do not presume to offer pictures of those dwellings again to the public. We have therefore, of set purpose, excluded entirely from this volume any of the conventional subjects, excepting only the picture of Independence Hall (page 120) without which a Pennsylvania book would be as incomplete as a Dutch garden without tulips.

THE OLD SHED DOOR—DELAWARE WATER GAP

HILLSIDE DECORATION—CHESTER

A WOODED MARGIN—LACKAWANNA

AN OLD DOOR—BETHLEHEM

ZIONSVILLE IN MAY

A GUARDED HOME——CHESTER

COME IN! — NEAR BOYERTOWN

A RETIRED VALLEY — CHESTER

We have, however, found, in the immediate vicinity of Philadelphia, a good many themes in which blossoms or streams appear. The cross roads in this vicinity, some of which are not yet improved, are still bordered by picket fences (page 14), and filled in spring with the aroma of apple blossoms. A little farther out, as in "A Pennsylvania Homestead" (page 18) there is the fascination of the farm drive, as we approach one of those self contained old centres of rural plenty. In Philadelphia itself, Cobb's creek is, in many of its aspects, most attractive. It is on pages 57, 292, and elsewhere. In the northeast part of the city is a pleasing old dam showing a church spire beyond (page 280).

We have followed the Wissahickon in all its windings. It is less sophisticated than the Schuylkill, and is deservedly known for the beauty of its banks as seen on page 58, and particularly on page 17, where the white cherry blossoms are poised lovingly on gracefully curved branches above the stream.

Philadelphia is unique among the cities of America, and perhaps the cities of the world, in that it contains many rural, or at least many semi-urban areas, such as the great tree with the cottage under its arms, on page 90.

Were not the estates about Philadelphia so generally made park-like, they would be far better for artistic purposes. We have shown an old homestead, or at least the restoration of one, on page 137 in a sketch.

So much can be made of gateways that we are glad to see the simpler sort in Pennsylvania, since they encourage citizens in general to attempt some aesthetic touches. "A Home Entrance at Reading" (page 210) "The Cottage Tree" (page 205) near Boyertown, "The Little L" near Zionsville (page 204), "The Picket Fence Row" and "The Gable Hidden in Blossoms" (page 196), a cottage almost completely hidden in bloom and beyond an old fence (page 184) and particularly "The Home Fence" (page 185), are examples which, found in particular about Zionsville, may be seen in somewhat similar form in many portions of the state.

"Over the Rail Fence" (page 165) and "Come In" (page 166), are both entrances to farms. Yet none of these examples shows the massive gate post of a place which too often gets its appellation of estate from the entrance alone.

Philadelphia has done much for America by its persistence in continuing the one family house. Modern methods of locomotion have assisted the city dweller so that he now may have this house in the midst of rural acres, or at least a rural half acre. We owe a great deal to those who, in the city of Philadelphia itself, or on its border line, have established places led to by the shadowed, fenced, and water bordered "Suburban Home Drive" (page 293).

The lover of his country must line up at once in protection of the home, a place where children may be reared in good air and in safety to their persons, and with at least an opportunity for development of sound minds in sound bodies. If we are to have an America worth housing and decorating, we must have families clothed and in their right minds. In their present largely unclothed condition, they can scarcely be supposed to be in their right minds. It would almost seem that the more available the means of providing clothing are, the less are those means used. Those with the least property seem to wear the most clothing. We seem to wonder whether it is the intention of vicious wealth to dispense with clothing altogether. Clergymen find this an awkward subject to deal with. They are either too modest to approach it or they feel the futility of doing so. Indeed, it seems to be only in the Catholic church that there is any courage in this respect. But without decency we shall soon be without homes, and without homes we shall soon be without a country. The Frenchman, the German, the Englishman and the American have built their literature, their thought, and their religion about the home. Careful students, however, have observed that love of home in China is far more intense than among our western races. It is a fair inference that as this family feature is the strongest characteristic of the Chinese, it has

[*Text continued on page 179.*]

THE OLD MILL RACE. *By Sladen after Nutting*

THE LEAP OF THE LEHIGH

By Mildred Hobbs

Into a terraced basin leaps
The Lehigh with a burst of song,
Free from the long
Monotonous confinement of its shore
Whose trees for many a mile
Leaned close with gentle sighs,
And where it could but murmur low and smile
Into the distant azure of the skies.
But over its trembling edge,
Free, with a sudden rush and roar,
Its waters plunge and leap in wild abandon —
Rough children out of school —
Into the whirling playground of a pool.
In iridescent clouds of foam they play,
In silver sheets
Torn to a thousand ribbons by the rocky ledge.
And clear against the cascades, snowy-churned,
With jewels flashing on her sunlit brow,
Sleeps the fair Goddess Liberty with face upturned
To catch the kisses of the river-spray.

How like a carnival of life it seems
When the blue current of the water breaks
To myriads of scintillating rainbow-flakes
Awhirl in the mad frolic of the falls!
They too return to drowsy murmurings and dreams
To carry on the purpose of the Giver.
How like all nature's wild things is a river,
Bounding with ecstasy when freedom calls!
Making majestic music of its symphony
To liberty!

A LEAP OF THE LEHIGH

ALL PRESENT! — MONTGOMERY

THE LITTLE CONESTOGA IN SPRING

SCHUYLKILL GRACE—READING

BRANDYWINE MEADOWS

A MAY PATH—BRANDYWINE

BRANDYWINE BOLES

OVER THE RAIL FENCE

WATER JOY—POCONO

BUTTONWOOD AND APPLE—CHESTER

A CONESTOGA BEND—LANCASTER

A CHESTER VALLEY

WINONA RAPIDS

LONG LAKE LIGHTS—WINONA

more to do with their immense vitality and the age-long continuance of their nation than any other one thing.

They are different from ourselves in this, also, that they make beauty a part of their worship; that they make pilgrimages sometimes daily for aesthetic reasons only, and that they set apart, as a sacred hour, the opportunity to caress with their eyes the things which God has made.

We depend upon Philadelphia to begin an American reform. There, where family meant more, perhaps, than elsewhere in America, let the family once more be exalted to its place as the beginning of religion and culture, of civilization and art. The people who do not love their homes will not long love anything else. If they are bored at home, everything eventually will bore them. When recreation becomes a business, and the home a barrack, we have reversed an order which lies deep in human nature, and which cannot be sucessfully contravened. The glorification of the home, externally and internally, as the shrine of a steady family love, is the first object of importance for patriotism and religion. Unless marriage means a family, it will not long mean a home. The interplay of human relations as they exist between various members of a family, big and little, supplies the only general available education in unselfishness. It is either home or anarchy. There is no middle ground. Any person without a powerful controlling motive of decency is dangerous if left at large. On the other hand, imprisonment has never, so far as we have scanned history, been a very successful beneficent influence. A good home in one's youth means less prison. At the last it will be found that the persons who don't go home, go to jail, or ought to do so.

To those who think these conclusions are strange, we would point out that it is the wandering foot that gets into mischief. We are ready to make a somewhat bold assertion, namely; that it is the moral duty of intelligent people to have beautiful homes. That is to say, if their loves are deep and their intelligence broad, they will study to decorate the home and its surroundings in such a manner as to afford no excuse for leaving it. The sordid motive of building rich houses and getting this and that sort of furniture because one's neighbors do the same, may thus be done away with, and the father and mother may give their attention to those elements of charm which provide cosiness. We have no good word to describe the resultant attraction from a combination of small, though cunningly devised grounds, walls, and furnishings. Bareness and sordidness are probably unnecessary in any American home. The crusade for attractive homes is the call of the age. If we could give up all our other special days and make every day an Old Home Day, we should discover that this matter lies at the bottom of our civic and social problems. If as much study were given to this question as to any other one of a dozen unimportant matters, the home life of America, now in danger, would become so much better than it is now as to empty most of the jails, fill the country with plenty, and working out from this one perfect institution, make all institutions perfect. If we ask ourselves how many of our institutions are substitutes for a home, we shall find that an ideal society, or even a moderate degree of approximation toward the ideal, would make unnecessary a great deal of our vicious institutionalism. Intemperance, immorality, insanity, theft, cruelty, and most of the other horrors come from bad homes.

One is never so much impressed with this fact as when one is seeking for daintiness or even picturesqueness along the countryside. There are plenty of large dwellings; there are plenty of dwellings, which, while not large, could be made attractive. But what one might call a picture house, which every house might be, is one of the rare things. Such a dwelling is really one of a thousand. When it is found, everyone pauses to look at it. We have in mind such a dwelling only one story in height, pictures of which by the hundred thousand have been eagerly sought all over the civilized world. This house could probably have been erected for a thousand dollars, certainly for much less than twice that sum. Millionaires look at it with envy. Almost as we write, one of the first men of wealth in our country has showed us pictures of a miniature country place where he and his wife dwell for eight months in the year, and which

[*Text continued on page 187.*]

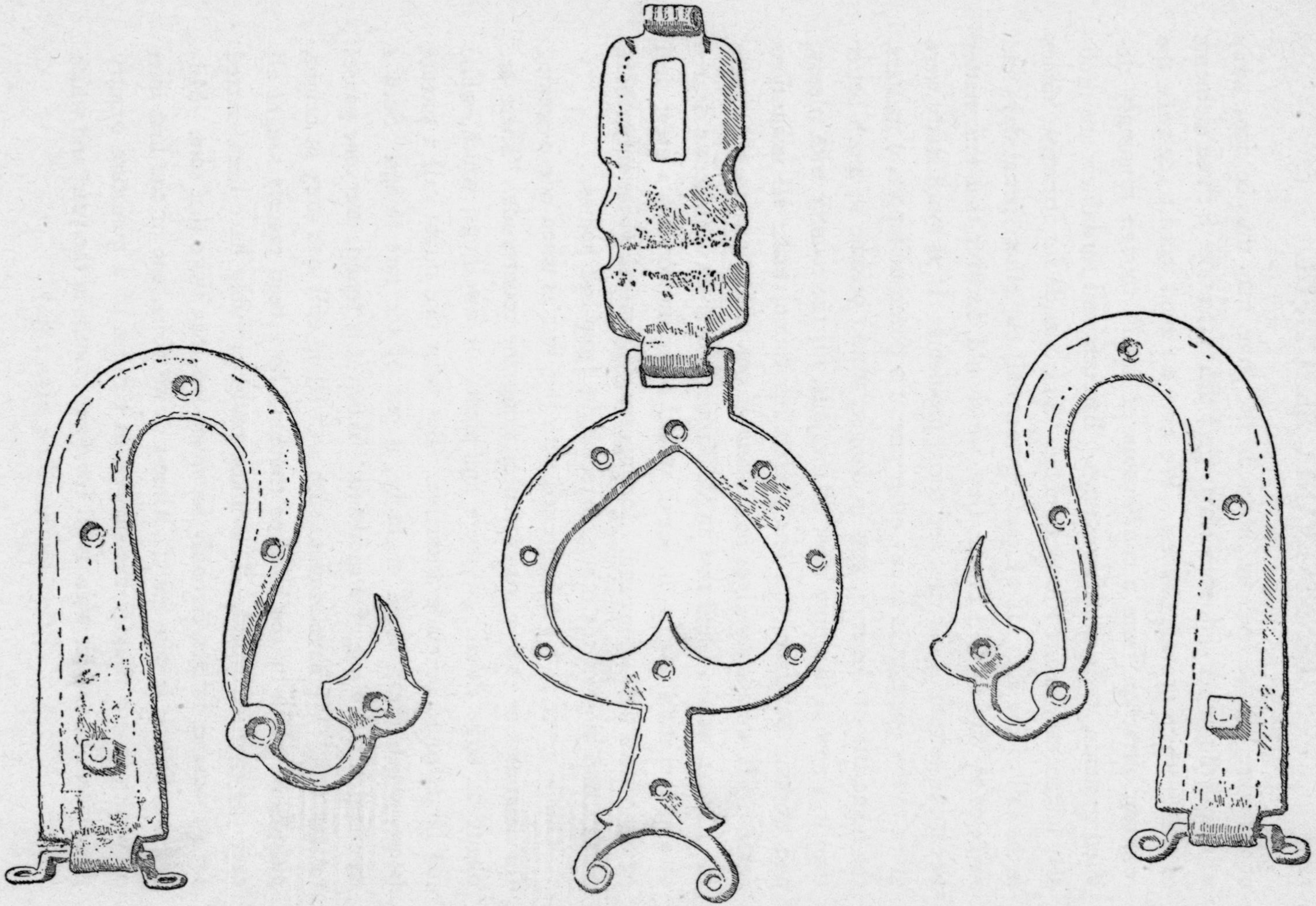

A SET OF CHEST HARDWARE

WHERE ROAD AND RIVER MEET

Written for the picture facing this page by MILDRED HOBBS

Little Road —
" Follow me over
*   The billowing hills*
*   Dotted with gardens*
*   And little stone houses,*
*   Past the wide acres*
*   Of buckwheat and corn,*
*   Past the green fields*
*   Where the golden herd browses! "*

Little Stream —
" Follow me into
*   The vale and the wood,*
*   Through the lush grasses*
*   Of velvety meadows.*
*   Come where the flute-throated*
*   Lark and the thrush*
*   Sing with the whispering*
*   Winds of the willows! "*

Little Road —
" Follow me, follow me,
*   Vagabond feet!*
*   Yours is no humor*
*   For bubbles and fountains!*
*   Follow me, follow me*
*   Over the hills,*
*   Far to the forest-filled*
*   Heart of the mountains! "*

A MILL IN THE DELL—CHESTER

PENN'S WOODS

A ZIONSVILLE BOWER

BROOK LOVERS—MONTGOMERY

THE HOME FENCE—ZIONSVILLE

A LEBANON COUNTY DRIVE

LANCASTER REFLECTIONS

absorbs a great deal of his time, because it holds his love. He takes far more pleasure in it than in his stately city dwelling. Nevertheless it is very slowly that people, otherwise intelligent, are learning to take up this important matter. There is still a quite general ignorance of the elements which constitute charm. There is almost no study of harmony except the harmony of colors.

We are, however, delighted to see the vigor of the efforts being put forth by so many to change current conditions. We even have a magazine devoted to the beauty of the home. Most magazines, in fact, have a department given over to that object. Whoever has any worth while ideas on the subject finds a ready hearing. It is inevitable that much that is crude and covetous should appear in this connection. Is there any aspect of life without its extravagances and dangers?

Thus we see small houses apparently erected to bid for the attention of home lovers, but covered with numerous useless gimcracks and spurious pretensions to old style. The expense is lavished where it isn't wanted and saved where it is necessary. All this is to be overcome through a more general study of the subject and a more careful making sure that what advertises itself as the desirable thing is really so. In other words, the toning up of general knowledge and the attention of the body of our people to this theme, becomes the engrossingly important matter of modern life. The question of well drained soils, proper outlook, good distance from the highway, ample ground, proper shade trees, simplicity of construction along well approved lines, the abandonment of pretension, the correlation of parts — all this, taken up in detail, forms not only the most profitable but one of the most interesting of studies.

THE CANALS OF PENNSYLVANIA

WHILE these canals are still used to a limited extent in the transportation of coal, they are getting more and more to feed the aesthetic sense, to supply Lover's Lane on the old tow paths, and to bring a touch of poetry into the counties through which they pass.

An old lock on the Delaware canal a dozen miles or so below Easton, shown on page 11 with its tow path, its watery highway, the high cliffs on the right, the fine shade trees and the distant lock and mill, seem to be more especially provided to feed our aesthetic sense than for any other purpose.

Some miles above New Hope, appreciative artists have gathered and made a seasonal colony on the canal. They have succeeded in glorifying beyond our common dreams the region of their choice. Their school house is one of their most successful achievements (page 253). The tree decoration along canals is the perfect opportunity for arching boughs to display themselves.

In many portions of the state the canals have become the most attractive features. They emphasize, of course, the height of a bluff, the depth of a valley, and the location of a village. Where, as often happens, they must cross a stream, their arches become a decorative feature. The spillways are miniature cascades. Particularly the numerous bridges which must cross the canals are the favorite resorts of boys who attempt to lure the darting fish.

If at last the span of patient mules be seen, driven by a youngster with a flapping straw hat, and towing a blunt-ended boat, deeply laden, the last charm is added to the drowsy effect. Every year improves the beauty of the canals. Would we might all grow old as gracefully! The rawness of freshly filled banks and the commercial exploitation which accompanied the building of canals has long since passed away. Only their poetry is left. The tow path is a ribbon road. Foliage encroaches everywhere.

A CHURCH AT BETHLEHEM

The inns, the dwellings, and even the storehouses and mills along the line have mellowed and softened and rounded and become covered with lichen or vines, and all things contribute to add the charm of romance to the charm of beauty.

A canal, however, is a constant reminder of the rapid manner in which the nineteenth century changed all outlooks and abolished old traditions. Since the beginning of time, civilization has found its first development on the shore of a canal. In Mesopotamia and Egypt, and also probably in Central America, a civilization arose in an irrigated country. The literature remaining which connects itself with the inception of canals predicted all sorts of national development from their use. No sooner, however, were they fairly under way than they became obsolete. Of a sudden, that mode of civilization was brought to an end. Within a brief time the feverish and even wildly thoughtless development of the trolley system in rural districts has also been found to be a mistake. Everywhere our smooth highways are a temptation for the development of a bus system. Undoubtedly we are moving along some other lines that will have to be abandoned. We live in an intensely changeful age and it becomes therefore highly important that we should seek to harmonize all this development with such attention to beauty as is possible.

We are glad that the trolley is passing away because we shall be rid of its poles and its noise, both of which are as nearly destructive to human peace as anything touching the senses can be.

BEAUTY SPOTS HERE AND THERE

A WOOD road partly grown up is one of the best things we know to feed the heart. One such is seen in "A Leaf Strewn Drive" (page 16). A drive along a small mill dam, as "A Lake Bank Drive" (page 18) is inevitably attractive because the changing stream and cloud, the jumping fish, and the varying colors of the foliage always have their

QUAINT WORK TABLE

message for us. A little north of Philadelphia, by the great high road, is the old homestead shown on page 21. The pear tree at its gable was enough to stop us. Its rambling out-houses, which do not here appear, gave a sense of plenty and picturesqueness.

Although we are not supposed to cross the Susquehanna westerly, we have shown just one picture made at Gettysburg. It is free of any touch reminding us of the battlefield.

On page 30 is a little by-road bordered by a rail fence with the slate posts of which we have spoken. We do not know whether these ever appear in the Old World, but certainly they are the most picturesque features for a field fence that we have ever seen in this country. The guide post reading "Tatamy — 4 mi." is an amusing instance of odd place names.

On the same page is shown the pleasing entrance of a community building of the Moravians in Bethlehem. It has a panel over the door in which is set a medallion and an historic record. One is permitted to wander through the interior of this building and to see the comfortable widows who are here furnished a home by the church. Up and down the corridors their doors stand open, and most of them make sweetmeats or fancy work to assist in their support. Their reverential life and quiet manner are a benediction.

On page 53 we show a fine "Old Chester Dwelling." Not that it is particularly different from others, but that it is an excellent type. It avoids the error noticeable in some Pennsylvania houses of the middle period, in that it possesses the fine large chimneys and the L as well as the main house. It is of stone neatly whitened. The residence is more pretentious than it seems, the most being made of the building and the grounds.

"The Harvest Field" (page 69) takes us into the very heart of the country in the golden autumn, with its piles of pumpkins, its shocks of corn, and its gable of the stone farm house with its large chimney, and with its fruit trees surrounding it. There is something about a pumpkin to make a rural poet of every man. The use to which we put the pump-

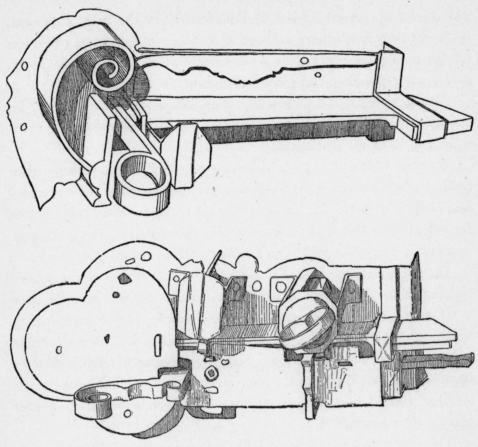

WROUGHT LOCKS

kin on All Hallows Eve, the comfortable lining which it supplied for our voracious stomachs in boyhood, its rich color, as it is scattered over a field, symbolizing the plenty of autumn, and even giving a superabundant richness of effect to the landscape, helped out by the peeping ears of corn of the same hue, are elements to set the mouth watering, if not the eyes. It is useless to reason that the pumpkin is the poor relation of the squash, to contend that it is merely fit for animals, to say that it is not a profitable crop and to make all manner of unkind remarks about it. Let us silence such folly. The pumpkin is the crown and jewel of good old country sentiment. Long may it decorate the old stone fence post at the back door, and prove the inspiration for every rural bard! We should be thankful for anything that is able to turn the mind from the exclusively practical. We have scarcely yet found "a soul so dead," as not to be aroused by the pumpkin. Logically or otherwise, it compels the old man to think of the girl whom he serenaded fifty years ago, of the fright he gave his chum by holding the jagged teeth and the gleaming countenance of the jack o' lantern at his window. What would American country life be without the pumpkin? It is a solace for most sorrows and casts a ruddy glow over the memory of a lost boyhood. Bearing these facts in mind, who shall say that the pumpkin does not pay? Whether we eat it or look at it or picture it, it seems quite adequate to stir the common man, and as Lincoln said, "there are so many of us." That man is fit for no good society who no longer loves a pumpkin. He wouldn't make a good husband, and his patriotism is a suspicious quantity. That colonial yellow, that oblate spheroid, that series of longitudinal lines which first vividly illustrated our childhood geography, that homely abundance and democratic nearness of the pumpkin, so free from the beloved modern word "exclusiveness" all hold us in thrall.

The David Rittenhouse birthplace restored, as it has been, by Mr. Ballard, and as shown on page 93, is now likely to be a permanent monument to the remarkable man whose name it bears. For heroism we have little need to look far. Even genius is discoverable, semi-occasionally. A high sense of honor is common. Fine scholarship is the mark of many Americans. A genial, social, and sweet nature is not far to seek. To find all these characteristics in one man, however, is almost miraculous. Who among us has not wished that Washington had been somewhat more of a scholar? and that this and that national worthy had possessed some missing element which we like to find in men? David Rittenhouse was unique in this country, in some of his abilities, and did and thought for his country for many years, though frail and often in great illness. When we consider the time at which he lived and the inventive genius he displayed, and think how he was, in the finer sense, self-made, and how his capacity

BUCK HILL FALLS

FARMERS' JOY

A BLOSSOMING GABLE—MONTGOMERY

A BRANDYWINE BRIDGE—CHESTER

THE OLD FARM—NEAR BOYERTOWN

CURVES OF THE CREEK—LUZERNE

YOUTH AND DREAMS——CHESTER

RIVER GRACE——SCHUYLKILL

and his character commended itself to his age and to successive generations, we feel that in Rittenhouse we have a fine type of an ideal American.

In the Delaware Water Gap, the most attractive scenery to us is not that which people go so far to view, but the little stream that flows through the village, bordered by quaint houses and overhung by shade trees or reflecting the blossomy spring (page 163).

At the edge of old Bethlehem is a stately dwelling now given over to neglect. We show the door (page 164). The sketch over the keystone, in the form of a carved tree like a sampler pattern, and the other dainty carving of the doorway, is carried out to a considerable extent in the cornice, not shown. It is a pity that this old dwelling, bought with a large tract of land by a corporation, could not be redeemed.

We love to find even in a village something like " The Cottage Tree " (page 205). In the double twist of the road here, and in a quaint bridge nearby, we find all the best elements which compose an English village, set down in a dear little valley near Boyertown.

The old forges of Pennsylvania are among the spots being visited by explorers. We have been furnished by Mr. Carl W. Drepperd of Lancaster with the picture of the ancient forge on page 218. Its over-shot water wheel marks it as an old timer. The tentative beginnings of the iron industry in Pennsylvania are surrounded with romance. They are the more interesting since they symbolize that dominant world-wide power and importance which America has acquired in this day through its unprecedented vast development of the iron and steel industry.

In " A Little Hill City " (page 248) we look down upon the valley of the upper Susquehanna at the village of the same name. It is for the most part a railway centre. Its setting, however, among the fine hills, is the most perfect that we have noted as an industrial location.

It is not often that we find the strawberry blossoms absolutely carpeting the earth, as on the stream bank picture (page 249). It is in Berks County, north of Reading.

To our thought, the " Twin Tree Homestead " (page 250) forms an almost perfect approach to a farm place. "The Ribbon Road" and the gentle upward slope with the overhanging blooms sheltering the dwelling is very satisfactory to the sentiments. The other picture on the same page, in a valley three or four miles west of West Chester, gives us the pleasure of a curve, a wall, and a slope with blossoms.

The country about Zionsville is most attractive in the spring as it appears in the pictures heading pages 260 and 261.

Swarthmore, near Old Chester, has a distinctive flavor always characteristic of college towns. The stream here has this year a wealth of foliage almost tropical. It appears on pages 267 and 291.

QUAINT UTENSILS

THE candle molds used in Pennsylvania were usually, like the other utensils of this state, designed to accomplish a great deal at once, but the earliest sort were single, as on page 225. These formed very large candles. A still earlier form, however, was the dipped candle. In Pennsylvania a very large reel was used from each of eight arms of which depended a wick. Each wick in turn was dipped in the hot tallow and the affair was revolved. By the time the circuit was made, the wick first dipped had hardened its tallow, and the process was repeated, the candle growing gradually and requiring a great many immersions.

The pie scallopers were developed in various quaint and even artistic forms owing to the fact that they were often gift pieces to sweethearts. At one end was an old fashioned cent filed into scallops, and at the other end there was a crescent shaped head with serrated edges. This end was used to pierce the dough to permit the gases to escape, and the other end was used to decorate the edge of the pie.

A most quaint work table originating either in Pennsylvania or New Jersey, is one of the writer's latest and most cherished acquisitions. On page 191 we give a sketch of it. The trestle frame going up in the form

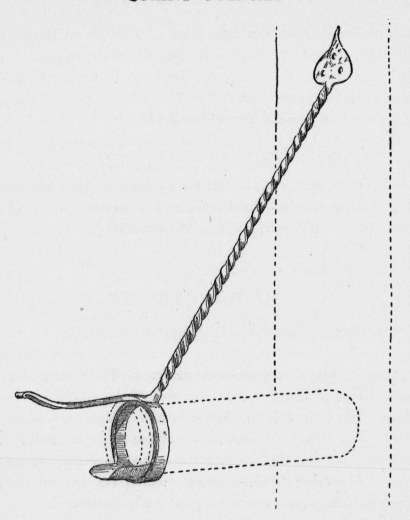

A TWISTED WROUGHT SPOUT BRACE

of steps, the central brace board with half-moon cut-outs, the hand holds
for the cubbies where the work was kept, and the rim formed about the
top by the molding, constitute one of the most interesting old pieces
imaginable.

A combination affair which might have proved convenient for an army
officer, and found at Bethlehem, is sketched on page 232. In the larger

[*Text continued on page 211.*]

ORCHARD BEAUTY

Written by MILDRED HOBBS for picture opposite

The orchard boughs are lost in tinted clouds
That hang like scarfs of lace upon the trees
As Spring unfolds her pollen-laden crowds
Of blossoms to the hummingbirds and bees.
Soft petals flutter on the air and strew
The windings of the lane with fragrant rose;
They sift among the grasses pearled with dew,
And drift above the dandelion-glows.

O fairy trees, most magic gift of spring,
How it is that in every blossom's place
The golden days of summer fail to bring
The crimson of an apple's ruddy face?
What wealth of bloom for beauty's sake alone
Is lavished on the old trees, petal-blown!

A PETALED CART PATH—CHESTER

THE LITTLE L—MONTGOMERY

NEW GREEN—LUZERNE

THE COTTAGE TREE—NEAR POTTSVILLE

CANADENSIS

A PAUSE AT THE BRIDGE

THE OLD STONE COTTAGE—NEAR VALLEY FORGE

BUCK HILL BOWL

COUNTRY CURVES—MONTGOMERY

OVERARCHED

THE BANK WALL—CHESTER

THE REVIVING YEAR—CHESTER

WHITE CHERRY LANE—NEAR READING

A HOME ENTRANCE—READING

end is a little ink well. Just above this section the long portion unscrews. That was as far as the seller got. He was considerably astonished when we unscrewed the little cap at the extreme top and drew out a pen knife from the long tube! Of course the pen knife, when we think of the name, was made expressly to mend the quill pen.

By the side of this quaint article we have sketched another fully as odd. It consists of a steel to strike on a flint. The back of this steel is so constructed with tail pieces as to form a pair of tweezers, by which the ignited tow was lifted and applied to a pipe bowl. This forms the smallest and quaintest pipe tongs that we have seen. It is only $1\frac{1}{4}$ by $3\frac{1}{2}$ inches.

A turned box suitable for holding the church warden pipe, and which we believe to be unusual is shown on page 225.

A series of latches, not hitherto published, and all of which were found in Pennsylvania, appears on page 223. The somewhat elaborate heart and dart pattern of the middle example, shows a strong feeling of taste. It will be noted that some of these latches have no bottom plate, but were made with a spur to be driven into the door, very much like the catch on a door jamb.

All the objects shown or mentioned in this book were found after the publication of the author's work *Furniture of the Pilgrim Century,* the later edition.

We know no greater pleasure on a rainy day than to wander through an old Pennsylvania homestead, both house and barn, and to see the processes which are or were carried on. The quilting frame, of course, was common to all early Americans, but the Pennsylvania housewife has clung to it more persistently than have her sisters in other states, so much so that she is even now often found making one more quilt. Of course it is not needed. It is only wanted. The creative spirit is active and can only be satisfied by making something, if it is merely a quilt. But some of these quilts are of no small importance. By the odd irony of practical life, the dwelling in which no quilt is being made is the dwelling where one is needed!

We did discover several persons who were capable of weaving, but we found no weaving being done except to satisfy the desire of some urban seeker after hand woven stuff. We have no doubt, however, that there are dwellings where weaving is yet being done for the mere love of it.

The knitting of heavy hose for men for winter use is not yet given up. It provides the only covering capable of giving comfort for out of door work in the cold weather.

We fear that the mechanical deftness of the iron worker is becoming extremely rare. The vast increase in the demand for cheaply made utensils in iron, and the giving up of the fireplace as a practical mode of cooking, have operated to throw the hand-forged utensils out of use. We inquired of various blacksmiths and found few who had ever seen the quainter old articles, and none who had ever made them.

A set of chest hardware, for instance, such as that shown on page 181, would antedate any living blacksmith. How full this old work is of a nameless charm. When a chest like this was in use, how much character it gave to the room in which it stood!

We presume that hand spinning of flax or wool has also completely passed out except in sporadic instances amongst the mountains. An odd reel such as that on page 213, used in Pennsylvania and New Jersey, has the peculiarity of a table at the centre of the revolving top. There is, of course, a mechanism which clicks to warn the winder that the full length of the skein has been reached.

FEATURES OF THE HOMESTEAD

ALTHOUGH the Pennsylvania barn was as a rule very large, the labors of the farmer usually overflowed it. He was then obliged to raise great stacks of straw, which added very much to the picturesqueness of a homestead. Sometimes even his hay was stacked to some extent. In this case, when the cattle were allowed to feed about it, the stack at-

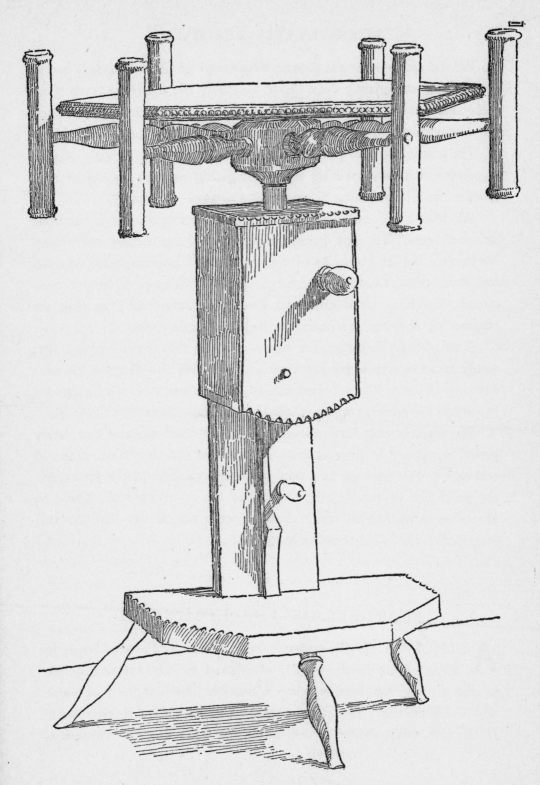

A REEL WITH TABLE

tained the shape of a vast mushroom, and was at once a shelter and a dinner for the animals.

The outbuildings of a farm house were among the more characteristic and pleasing features. The well was not seldom completely housed in, and was operated by a windlass superseded by a pump in later times. Long open sheds protected the farm vehicles. Walls as massive as the fortifications of a feudal castle are still to be found surrounding some of the barnyards. We remember one instance where the yard lay at the edge of a steep valley, and where the wall has run up some twenty feet. It really looks like a bastion! These people built for the generations. They had the family spirit almost as strongly marked as among the Chinese and, living in a country free from earthquakes and with abundant building material, they patiently laid their stones without regard to their size.

The ducks and geese formed a considerable part of the wealth of the farm. Their products were a perquisite of the housewife. The custom of keeping large flocks of aquatic fowls was continued from the Old World. The immense and innumerable feather beds that resulted are a feature of the country place. There were enough feather beds so that every member of the household could have several under him and one over him! And all of the finest down!

Of course, in the old days the sheep furnished the clothing for the family. The wool was washed while it was still on the sheep's back, and carding, spinning and weaving were all done at home. Even the leather was sometimes tanned in private vats or if not so, there was a tannery not far away. It furnished not only material for shoes and boots, but for leather aprons, for harness, for upholstery and numerous other purposes. A huge settee has recently been found on the very high back of which was stretched, as on a frame, great broadsides of cow hide, and more covered the seat. The newness of the country and the community life of some of the religious bodies which were opposed to the purchase of what could be made, all tended to the enhancing of that home charm which arises when local fashions predominate.

A BLOSSOMY AISLE—CHESTER

ROADSIDE DRAPERY—CHESTER

LONG BUTTONWOOD ARMS—LITTLE CONESTOGA

'TWIXT STREAM AND BLOSSOM—CHESTER

AN ANCIENT FORGE

THE WHITE KNOLL—LANCASTER

We haven't mentioned the cheese making on the farm which, to a comparatively recent time, was continued and, in odd corners of the state, is still carried on. Cheese was a very important factor in diet in the olden times, when the herd occupied a larger place in domestic economy than it does at present. This fact is hinted at in such old English phrases as " bread and cheese."

The presses and other processes of cheese making required a rather cumbersome outfit. These things were often kept in a room apart. The dairy was sometimes attached to a spring house, where the water could be dipped up by the pailful as it issued from a living source, and flowed into a reserve basin. One who has never had the joy of coming upon a cheese making, and being invited to partake of the fresh curds, has lost a memorable experience.

Thus one who would see a farm in being, where everything is carried on in a businesslike manner, may reach the goal of his quest in Pennsylvania. The farmer himself is large and strong, and so are his wife and children. All the buildings were large, all the vehicles and tools and processes attained the most ample size. The Conestoga wagon would hold twice as much as a New England wagon. The farmer in the field carried on no one-horse enterprise. Whereas, in many other parts of the country, especially northeast of Pennsylvania, a span of horses was the goal of ambition, four or perhaps more often six horses were attached to the great freight wagons, and the processes of plowing and other field work were carried on by three and four horses abreast. We have seen the four so working in this very year. They remind one of the Roman quadriga.

It is easy to understand how a certain contempt has become habitual toward farm life. The degenerate farm offers a keen mark for ridicule. The farming carried on in the ample way seen on the fine plains of Lancaster and Bucks and many other fertile counties can only excite the respect of the beholder.

CHANGES IN PENNSYLVANIA LIFE

THE unprecedented growth of coal and iron mining and the immensity of the steel industry are operating to change the life of Pennsylvania. Indeed, the change has proceeded already to such a marked degree that only in the country is life at all what it used to be. The cognate manufactures, stimulated by the wealth of iron and steel, the immense demand for brick and cement, the latter of which is really bringing in a new era, carry forward still further the modifications of life in Pennsylvania. The question before us is how to make use of this development so that it shall not destroy the best of the past, but may be availed of to build up a twentieth century life agreeable to an aesthetic ideal. For, trailing after the practical, sometimes, it is true, at a sad distance, comes the ideal. One generation pours the ingots and another generation considers how to reshape the crude material into a harmonious civilization. It is inevitable that during this period of change much that is ugly shall appear. The foreign cast that has been given many districts in Pennsylvania, where the people and their language are hard to understand, presents, of course, to the social student, his problem, and to us the question of physical expression in landscape architecture and art that is to be wrought out by the new generation.

There seems to be no doubt that our dwellings, as well as our roads, are to be of cement, or of stucco covering tiles. We have to consider what sort of edifice, in an aesthetic way, can be created from these materials. We immediately look to Italy for an answer to this question. Travelers are accustomed to go into ecstasies over the color of Italian edifices. As a matter of fact, most of them have no color beyond a white or a whitish gray, and when they are colored, they are frequently of a very offensive tint. A soft yellowing is the most natural effect to be hoped for. But when, as in Italy, we often see brilliant blue or green or other strange colors, we hope that there will be a sufficiently powerful influence in

A DECORATED WEAVING STOOL END

this country to prevent painting it blue. Aside from the color, the question of form must largely settle itself as regards simple cottage architecture, because it will not be feasible to secure, without too much expense, desirable shapes in cornices and otherwise. We can at least hope that the roofs may be slated rather than covered with metal. The question of the walls may perhaps best be solved by the growth over them of vines. The danger of allowing vines to grow over stone work and of disintegrating the joints does not arise in a cement dwelling. Vigorous local propaganda for the decoration of cement dwellings is one of the practical ideas suggested.

Then, as to the gardens, it is a question whether generations of education will encourage sufficiently the creation, within walls, of simple flower decorations. Even the descendants of the English families in America have largely abandoned the little garden in front of the dwelling, so that we need not be surprised if it is very difficult to revive that habit among ourselves, and still more difficult to inculcate it among those who have recently come to live here.

The question of highways is being settled rapidly, but a very eagerly pursued effort to induce the building of dwellings back from such highways, is not yet in evidence. Was it ever known that this desirable object was taught in school? We have seen coal districts in Pennsylvania with passably well located and well built houses. This proves that the thing can be done. The surroundings of those houses are not yet at all beautiful. Perhaps it will be a hundred years before they become beautiful. By that time some different method of heating must come to the fore. Any change in that respect must be for the better. If we learn to extract means of warmth from chemical combinations derived from the air, or from other now unused sources, the presumption is that less dirt will be connected with the process than that which surrounds the word coal.

The rapid rise in the price of fuel, despite the use of fuel oils, which some supposed would stabilize prices, should be a strong stimulant to the lover of the beautiful, that he may consider the effect upon the external aspects of a community. The possible use of electrical heat may at length

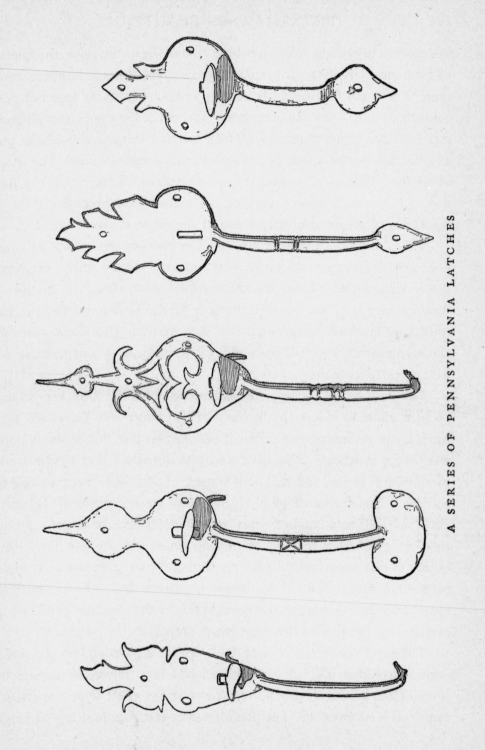

be a priceless advantage to the aesthetic side of life. Dust, while responsible for beautiful sunsets, is also responsible for too many other things which we gladly leave without description. Given a home without dust, and the battle for the beautiful is more than half won. We shall be encouraged to construct finer forms both within and without the dwelling, if we can feel some assurance that they will not become unsightly on the surface.

Public building and municipal constructions of all sorts are going forward at an alarming pace just now. We say alarming because the ease with which money can be borrowed has saddled upon communities debts such that taxes must be an almost killing burden for generations. Nevertheless the expenditure may, in the added convenience of locomotion, and in the stimulus to local pride, be worth while.

RACIAL ELEMENTS AND AESTHETICS

PENNSYLVANIA is richer in the best racial elements than is any other state. The Swedes and the Dutch were the first settlers. The Germans of various religious organizations like the Moravians, and the French Huguenots followed. Then, of course, there was the very large element of English people who came with Penn or on his invitation. We have here, therefore, the five finest racial elements, both as regards character in general and the aesthetic arts in particular, if we omit the Italian.

The Swedish people, it is true, did in some instances find life made too hard for them, and returned to the old country. Sweden is rather notable for the application of art in carving to domestic architecture and furniture. The Dutch also have the same well deserved reputation. The Germans were from a region where wood carving and iron work has long been a vogue. The French are naturally an artistic people. The English people, while not notably susceptible to beauty, nevertheless have in their domestic architecture a high repute for the character of their dwellings, as regards size, comfort, and substantiality.

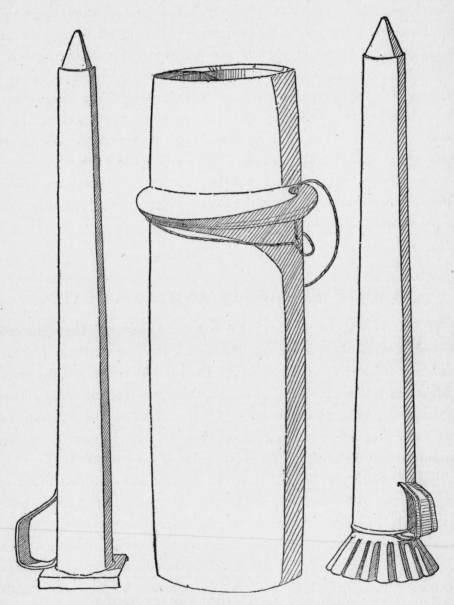

A PIPE TUBE AND CANDLE MOLDS

We have, therefore, in Pennsylvania, a very remarkable assemblage of races which should have produced a fine development on the aesthetic side. The hindrance to such a development was the segregation of races for a long time. The religious tenets of a great many of the settlers tended to keep them apart from their neighbors of the same race, and still more from their neighbors of other races. The development was rather intensive than broad. Also the lack of good roads set communities off by themselves. Then, whatever we say of the merits of the Germans immigrants, which were many and substantial, we cannot say that they entertained gladly new ideas from other races. If they had a fault, it was in a certain self-sufficiency which led them to believe that their own society was ideal. In fact, it was intended to be ideal from their point of view.

The Friends were given to trade and manufactures rather than to agriculture. They were the townspeople rather than the farmers. If they owned farms, they were more apt to carry them on at second hand, or to use them as summer resorts than otherwise. The Swedes also, for the most part, lived by themselves. Altogether there was an unusual and peculiar segregation of the different parts of the Pennsylvania colony, which meets its counterpart nowhere else in America.

We should take note that the real settlement was on the banks of the Delaware, on both sides and for a long distance. The Wilmington district, in fact Delaware as a whole, was counted as a unit with Penn's colony for some time, but it never relished the proprietary government and early sought separation. The same may be said in some respects of the West Jersey settlement.

The Friends themselves, owing to their attitude on war, were often sharply at variance with the other colonies and with the king. Penn's house at Pennsbury was very fine for its day, and many of the Friends early acquired comparative wealth and imported luxuries from England. There was, however, a marked lack of homogeneity. Also, there was variance in the colony itself. All these reasons, together with others which we cannot trace, hindered any marked development of the aesthetic side of life, or a

DELAWARE WATER GAP

THE MIDST OF THE ORCHARD

THE TURBULENT BRODHEAD

THE WASHINGTON CHURCH, VALLEY FORGE

THE TWO ARCH BRIDGE—NEAR BOYERTOWN

A MOUNTAIN RIVER—POCONO

LAKE AND HILL

communication of ideas of beauty from one part of the colony to another.

It is very likely that we should attribute to the Swedes the carving, or at least the shaping, or many articles of use or adornment in the home. To the Dutch, also, we certainly owe what is called the Frisian element in carving. We should here distinguish sharply between the small and very early element of Dutch settlers, and the larger, later and general settlement of Germans. The German objects to being thought of as Dutch, though from our American point of view the diligence and spirit of liberty and the other steadfast qualities of the Dutch place them as high in our estimation as any other race whatsoever, not excepting the English. We can easily understand, however, that the Germans, in the interest of truth, should be known as Germans. Not only so, but they are for the most part of the pre-Revolutionary time, and the ruling element among them came over in the seventeenth century, or very early in the eighteenth. Germantown, which they founded, is sufficiently old and important to serve as an unmistakable and lasting monument. Particularly it is a curious and unkindly error to confuse them with the Hessians, who settled here after their capture or after their discharge from the English service. We do not find that the Hessians exercised any very marked influence in the development of Pennsylvania.

Gathering up, then, the threads of the different races, we consider that in the domestic arts and their development, as evidenced in the tools and the architecture which have remained, the Swedes, the Dutch, and the Germans all contributed, but the last in a greater degree than the other two together. As to the French element, no doubt some part of the alertness and vivacity of the Huguenots entered into the life of Pennsylvania, but we doubt if this influence was large.

The dominant influence in the larger towns was apparently English. It is true that the Germans soon developed cities from villages, or at least their towns reached a size sufficient to give them a somewhat urban character.

We do not observe that the English settlers contributed to the domestic

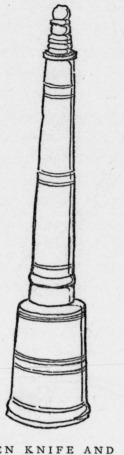

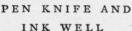

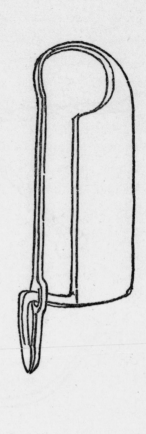

PEN KNIFE AND   PIPE TONGS AND
INK WELL   STEEL

arts or architecture to a great extent, in the sense that they gave anything
new or peculiar to America. They did build in their towns and even on
their country estates very solidly, but they followed, just as the Germans
did in their architecture, the English traditions. There was an inevitable
modification of English traditions arising out of the materials at hand in
Pennsylvania. Sometimes we are told with considerable gusto that the
bricks of this or that house came from England. If this were always a
fact, it would not indicate that the building was also purely English in style,
or that it was any better for that. Bricks were brought sometimes as ballast,

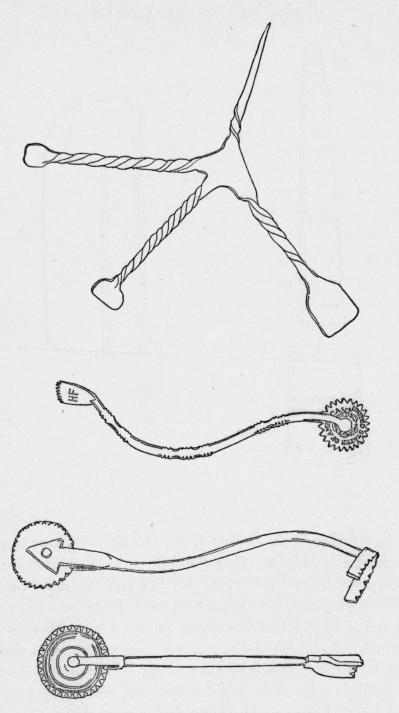

PIE SCALLOPERS AND BUTTONHOLE CUTTERS

perhaps. If not, there was no necessity for bringing them, as all·the materials were more readily at hand here. The architecture was, of course, mostly practical, but more fine public or semi-public buildings existed in Philadelphia at one time than in any other American city.

In the domestic art in the later period such men as Savery stood at the head. Of course the preeminence of Stiegel is well recognized, perhaps too well. By this we mean that the vogue of his glass has proceeded to an extreme. For there were other good makers and undoubtedly it is true, in his case as in that of the great furniture makers, that his name and style is applied broadly to much with which he had no immediate connection. Nevertheless his beautiful work was spread in great quantities, not only through Pennsylvania, but in other states where he had warerooms. We notice even now, in some villages of Pennsylvania, that glass work, particularly the cut glass work, is carried on. In pottery and china the attraction of Trenton has been so strong, for reasons connected with the abundance of material, and the possible accidental presence of certain artists there, as to draw away from Pennsylvania much work of this sort. Indeed, Trenton now claims, and probably with justice, to be the greatest world center in china and allied manufactures.

Philadelphia was an early center of the chair industry. The excellence and early character of Pennsylvania work in walnut we have mentioned. The extent of it we have not fully scanned. Pennsylvania made furniture very largely, not only for itself, but for contiguous states like New Jersey, Maryland, and even Ohio. A certain style established itself here in the mahogany period. It was marked by dignity, solidity, and good craftsmanship. The beautiful walnut of Pennsylvania has been eagerly sought in New England, New York, and the west by collectors in these later years. The diversified manufactures of Pennsylvania in which the arts of design or other elements of beauty enter, are very extensive and now go to the ends of the earth. Their rugs and their carpets, their art brick, and the thousand branches of manufacture indicate a keeping alive of the love of beauty which is the honest inheritance of the Pennsylvanian.

THE PLACID RIVER—PERKIOMEN

A CHESTER DELL

THE WEE POOL—LANCASTER

A LITTLE LANE—MONTGOMERY

THE BRODHEAD AT PLAY

THE OPEN VALLEY—CHESTER

CHERRY LANE—LEBANON

PAST CASTLE WALLS—POCONO

ASPEN RAPIDS—POCONO

LANCASTER MEADOWS

LATE BLOSSOMS—MONTGOMERY

HOMESTEAD BEAUTY—MONTGOMERY

THE LITTLE CONESTOGA

YOUNG LEAVES—POCONO

COMPANIONS—CHESTER

A HAZY MIRROR—LEHIGH

The fine arts in Pennsylvania have, it is probable, come to the fore somewhat more than in other states, with the possible exception of New York and Massachusetts. Not a few have lavished their wealth freely on the collection of the most splendid known paintings that were available. By recent decision of the powers that be, a stately museum in Fairmount Park is soon to be completed, which may serve as a beautiful and dignified center of public art treasures. The Philadelphian, who has always emphasized the home, has adorned it with discrimination. Our work leads us to scan, for the most part, the rural, or at least the external beauties of the state. We rejoice in the immense field of the fine arts as they have been recognized and developed in Philadelphia. We may hope that Pennsylvania artists will devote still more attention to the peculiar merit of Pennsylvania kitchens. The very popular and always delightful products of Dutch painters are largely concerned with sweet domestic scenes. Art owes something to history, and it would be a sad omission, should the present age pass away without adequate artistic records of the homely life in America of the village and the farm, indoors and out. The landscapes will always be with us, but the peculiar features of the domestic economy are fast passing away, and the architecture of the old time will soon follow it. Artists have every incentive to produce delightfully characteristic paintings of the kitchens, living rooms, courtyards, and barns of Pennsylvania, as they appear in the Moravian and other distinctive neighborhoods.

The objection to luxury on the part of some of the societies of immigrants, doubtless worked against the production of anything for beauty's sake alone. This very fact, however, restricting their artistic instincts to the adornment of necessary articles, probably stimulated art in the home instead of choking it. Where else in America can we find articles as quaint or interesting, or with as much personality in them, as about the Moravian settlements? Probably no one outside of Pennsylvania will record adequately these distinctive things. If it is done at all, it must be by Pennsylvania artists who, being on the ground, are most conveniently able to do this work. Further, their own ancestry and training should naturally stimulate them to a desire to record the native craftsmanship.

We may fairly presume that the resources of Pennsylvania, artistic, financial, and patriotic will, in the coming generation, gather into their museums the finest specimens of work in the eighteenth century. Not only so, but we may hope, possibly we should expect, that sufficient influence will be brought to bear on the development of Pennsylvania to secure a far greater degree of uniformly good construction and adornment than has yet been reached. The wealth of Pennsylvania is incredibly great. It would be necessary to use but a small part of it to enchance, in an immense degree, the aesthetic attractions of the state.

ROADS AND PARKS

TOWARD the important end on which we have been dwelling, the development of roads and parks will greatly contribute. We do not know whether America fully appreciates what a real revolution has come about in its roads during the last twenty years. In the extent of miles of road built, in their breadth and solidity, there has never been, in the world's history, so stupendous an expenditure. The greatest wars in human history, except the last war, did not represent such an outlay. The resources of generations in some districts have been tied down for these improvements. Nothing short of a rage for roads has manifested itself. Had anyone said a score of years ago that billions of dollars would be expended in a

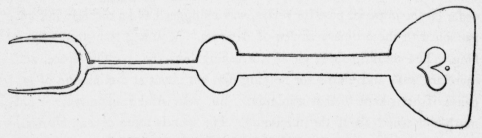

COMBINATION COOKING UTENSIL

short time on highways, he would have been considered one more visionary. Had anyone said that the cost per mile of these highways would far
exceed the cost of railroads, when they were built, he would have been
thought a candidate for a madhouse. Yet all this is just what is happen-
ing. Certain large districts in the south at once extricated themselves from
hub-deep clay and stand on permanent cement. We have previously mentioned that this is to be a cement age in architecture. Still more is that
to be a fact as regards highways. The stone walls of America are literally disappearing in the roads. Large hills are being eaten away. Deep
valleys are filled, gorges are crossed, stupendous cuts are made through
the hills, curves are eliminated and many of the most remote country districts are placed within a few minutes' spin of all that men have previously been obliged to take a day or two in procuring. The historian of the
next century will be obliged to state that the twentieth century was the
age of road building. He would be daring who should limit the billions
that are yet to go into roads in America. For the process is really only
begun. In the south, the middle west, and the mountain regions one still
sees that development is contingent upon roads to come. Already the
rivalry of the public highway with the railway has excited much attention.
Only the development of the country can support both on a sound basis.

This era of building, with wealth and raw materials and a demand all
unprecedented, is doing more to call out the thought of the average citizen to the beauty of his country than all other agencies combined. John
Smith and his capable little car can go anywhere, and he means to go almost
everywhere. A Roman officer of high rank, in his chariot, and with an
order on the imperial post for relays, was a sluggard and a plebeian in comparison with the ordinary citizen of America. Mounted in his car, he is a
king. The municipalities vie in furnishing him free parking space, and
there are ways and means for helping him get about at a minimum of expense, if he is kept to that minimum. But your American traveler is not
much concerned about the minimum. He spends more abroad than all
other travelers together, and at home what he spends can never be com-

puted. With his wife, and perhaps a boy whose eyes are just beginning to take in the meaning of life, he sweeps up into the passes of the mountains and skirts the great lakes and rivers of his country. He sees the various forms of architecture. Vast bridges, steamships, mines, edifices pass before his delighted gaze. As the average man will not read, or at least will not read anything of much consequence, the educative value of seeing the world can scarcely be overestimated. Perhaps two or three journeys a year of this sort are worth all the schooling which the boy will get. Certainly it will illustrate and enchance the value of the schooling which he has received, and bring him back to his books far more alert than when he left them.

We do not overlook the economic and social evils arising from a motor mad public. We are here, however, taking stock of the favorable features connected with the new spirit of travel. People are learning geography by illustration. The mountains and the sea about which they have read are now before them. Whatever advantages accrue from intercommunication are certainly pouring in on the present day American. The old time education of a well-to-do youth in England included a continental tour. The American citizen does not even require a competency to undertake a more extensive journey. Even as regards foreign journeys, there are annually crossing the great water, eastwardly, something like a hundred times as many persons as Washington had in his army at Valley Forge. We may lament that they do not bring back more from their journey. Let us be glad for what they do bring back. Of course the test of an education is the value of a man's observations in a given time. But it is useless to presume that a person without broad culture will return from any journey with any considerable part of the store of valuable information possible to gain with a better equipment. The very journey itself is in the nature of supplying that equipment. The next journey will mean more to the same individual. None of us are so well educated but that we see new truth and beauty breaking forth every day from something at which we have worked all our life long. If any man sees a hun-

CHAD'S FORD BRIDGE

A CHESTER BYWAY

A LITTLE HILL CITY

A FISHING SEAT—CHESTER

A CHESTER ROADSIDE

STRAWBERRY MEADOW—CHESTER

TWIN TREE HOMESTEAD—LUZERNE

CURVES OF BEAUTY—CHESTER

dredth part of the beauty or meaning of anything, he is seeing a very great deal. The noblest and the greatest mind is only beginning. The pride of intellect is the most common and the most shameful of any form of pride. We see in children of ten a vast contempt for the ignorance of children of seven. This is true of children of a larger growth.

The roads are to be our most hopeful educators. They are the common school of the world awheel. We shall see how other people live. One of the finest and most optimistic aspects of travel is found in the fact that we can scarcely find a new evil by traveling, but we can find much good that is new. Evil has a way of becoming cosmopolitan, like the small pox and the plague. But we must go over the hill and we shall find a new beauty. In the next state we shall see a better way of doing what we have been doing less well. In other lands we shall note customs and applications which are good but alien to us, yet worthy of adoption. If we can constantly remember that almost all knowledge is comparison, it is obvious that travel is fitted to increase knowledge more rapidly than any other means. A few years ago the high school graduates were in the habit of making a little expedition to Washington. It was our American tour of the continent from Main Street. So far as it went, it was excellent. A shut-in train, fog, smoke, the night and the back doors of cities, which are mostly seen on railways, did, however, occupy a great deal of the journey. Our main motor roads, however, pass over the better portions of our country. The immensity of the sea and its call to an undeveloped nature, and the solitude of mountains, awake the poetic instinct and broaden the imagination. The works of men as seen in travel lead us to think less of the importance and the merit of our own work. Thus travel is both stimulating and humbling. The imitative faculty is stirred by seeing what others do. Even a Chinaman is benefited by travel. The perfection of his art along certain lines has been such as to cause, if not to justify, a complacent satisfaction with his own civilization. The same fact is measurably true in parts of America.

In spite of the largely transient and superficial impressions derived

A LAFAYETTE COLLEGE HALL. *By Sladen after Nutting*

A SCHOOL AT NEW HOPE

by travelers who are not students, it is inevitable that a diffusion of information beyond precedent is to result from the improvement of roads. The very fact that men are willing to vote the funds for building these roads speaks something of the purpose to which they intend devoting such improvements. They intend to bring to their homes the best of what appeals to them of what they see in their journeys. It is a peculiarly American trait to consider that nothing is too good for the American family. He is a poor farmer or mechanic as well as a poor American, who does not think his own son and daughter worthy of a training such as the children of the wealthy receive. The larger public schools that will result from good roads, will have their merits and demerits, but we hope that the good will overtop the bad.

The timid may say that it is time to call a halt in road building. Do they remember that we have not yet a decent highway, and some of the time not even a passable highway, from the north to the south, and from the east to the west? Particularly in Pennsylvania, where the land is so rich, the roads are bound to be poor except where modern construction has taken hold of them. A probable solution of what must be done with the heavy clay roads threading many rich districts in Pennsylvania, will be the construction of narrow roads of macadam leading to the trunk lines. Pennsylvanians think that at present New England is in advance of them in road building. The natural materials in New England often lie on the road itself; in fact, many of the roads, being of gravel, scarcely require building. Our own judgment, after traveling over a multitude of Pennsylvania roads, is that the state is doing very well in its road building. It is true that some of the trunk lines are rather narrow. Now that vehicles are passing all the time, a double track is a continual necessity. However, where this is not feasible a hard even if rough bed at the sides of the finished highway is the proper solution. It prevents the necessity for a wide construction, which would be prohibitory on subordinate lines.

It is most interesting to observe how certain districts, hitherto so remote as not to be known, are coming into public favor.

MENNONITE CHURCH, NEAR COOPERSBURG

PARKLIKE PENNSYLVANIA

THE parks about Philadelphia are larger, or seem larger, than those about any other city. Also the natural beauty of the Schuylkill and the Wissahickon are such as to provide natural in addition to culture attractions. Many miles of softly charming aspects or of bold high bluffs are seen in the park environs of Philadelphia.

The house of William Penn, a curious construction, valuable principally for historic reasons, has been set up in Fairmount Park. Other old dwellings have been preserved. The city fathers had a long prevision when they provided these beautiful spaces, so decorated with trees and streams.

Of late the extension of the park idea to the Roosevelt Boulevard, and in other directions, has been a stupendous work. Philadelphia is the most difficult city, in its retail district, in which to get about, that we know, but it is the most delightful city in its environs, to circuit. One may literally travel for days without seeing all that is worth while in the natural beauties of Philadelphia itself. We have, of course, omitted most of the park "views" since they are done to death. But they are no less beautiful on that account. The planning of the drives and walks has engaged a great deal of attention for many years. Constant accessions are made, and the Cobb's Creek district particularly has been lately developed.

Let a metropolitan district as large as Philadelphia once begin to park its suburbs, the urge to go forward will be felt from various directions. One constantly says to oneself, "If this last stretch can be made so beautiful, why not carry it farther out into the country?" We have only to extend the fever of road building a little, to make it a fever of beautiful parking. Happily even the selfish interests of those who wish to dispose of land help to forward the beautifying of the roadsides. The impetus being once given, we may hope that the natural beauties of Pennsylvania may tempt to a vast system of beautifying the whole state. We understand that there is at present a corporate obstacle to the improvement of the stretch of road at the Water Gap. The public interest is too great to be thwarted here permanently. We hear that a long stretch of road on the Baltimore Pike towards Wilmington has been made feasible through private interest. At least we see that it has been completed worthily.

Road building in Pennsylvania is not easy. There are many sharp pitches to overcome, necessitating permanent grades that are of doubtful wisdom owing to their steepness, or immensely expensive detours. The valleys of Pennsylvania run in long, sweeping lines, so that to cross from one to another often means a formidable climb. This is true from Bethlehem south. Of course we look for conditions like these throughout the mountain districts. But everything that is worth while being done, will be done sometime. So vigorous has been the beginning, and so urgent is

SPOON RACK, BETHLEHEM

the spirit of the age, that we feel certain of a very general network of permanent roads through the country. Whether the country will have anything left to foot the bill, we are not so sure. Perhaps, when we are gone some other race may enjoy the works of the present harassed generation.

The system of connecting the parts of various cities by boulevards has in some instances, in America, reached a broad application. Happily, no one metropolis works alone. The teeming cities reach out their hands to one another and are gradually being linked by the gray, dustless highways. One who has come in from New York south of Binghamton through splendid roads that pass through Scranton and the south, will feel that his advantages over the previous generation are immense.

The Philadelphian may drive to New York City, to Pittsburgh, to Williamsport, to Lancaster, under conditions so favorable for health and charm that he may be grateful for life in the twentieth century. As much, however, as all this means to him, the dweller in a smaller city is still more grateful.

In seeking to make the district traversed by these roads parklike, we hope the mistake will not be made of over-refining the natural landscape. This has been done too much in the past. Many natural beauties have been spoiled because men took it for granted that they must imitate the cut turf of England in the more level counties. We see enough of cut turf about our own lawns to be glad to escape from it. A more careful negligence, if we may use the phrase, will prove far more grateful to the aesthetic sense.

A large measure of the benefit of roads is seen in the improvements which they stimulate on private grounds. Most citizens feel a certain pride that their premises shall be presentable. When they find themselves suddenly upon a beautiful modern highway, the happy impulse is to be rid of the ugly features about their premises. The real use of a park is not to be found in itself alone, but rather in inducing persons on their private grounds to carry out the spirit of the park improvements. We have in mind a section of the parks in Providence, where lawns blend into the public grounds without any visible line of demarcation. In fact, the writer, dwelling in such a location, was often delighted by seeing a public flock of sheep coming up to his own window. All public improvements are stimulated by men of taste and patriotism. Other men, seeing this large object lesson, catch by reflex action, the spirit that has prompted parks. Of course, the outcome must sometime be a parklike state and a

A FOREST TUMULT—POCONO

THE ASCENT BY THE FALLS—LUZERNE

HOME IN SIGHT—ZIONSVILLE

A POCONO FRESHET

A PENNSYLVANIA WASH HOUSE

A DELAWARE TOW PATH—NEW HOPE

AN ARTIST'S CANAL—ABOVE NEW HOPE

parklike country, wherein all outlooks shall be cleared of whatever is unsightly and beauty, either in a wilder or a more finished mood, shall appeal alternately and constantly to every traveler. The world is good enough, if we would not spoil it. It is unnecessary to improve on nature. We have only to be taught by her. It is in the great and populous states like Pennsylvania that this necessary beginning of an aesthetic world must be made. Where multitudes are well educated, and multitudes more are wealthy, we shall fairly expect long strides to be made toward a world all beautiful. Just at present this ideal may seem to lie an immense distance away. We do not so think of it. Beginnings are always difficult, and what glorious beginnings have been made! We are doing things today along aesthetic lines and without much difficulty which would have required the propaganda of years to set in motion, a decade ago.

GETTING THINGS DONE

THE difficulty of getting great things done is merely a difficulty of education. The rapid diffusion of education by means of the newspaper, and even by the radio, encourages us to believe that the great body of the people can be induced to do greater things more easily than in the past. During the great war, there was a readier acceptance of the draft than has ever occurred in a previous instance in human history. This means, of course, a very strong and general taking hold by the people at large of good ideas. Consider the difficulty that arises in a small state of getting great things done. The lack of resources prevents a world wide taking up of a grand idea. In America let a great purpose once seize the great editorial writers, it will not be long before that purpose will be placed for contemplation in the homes of all Americans. The world has served its apprenticeship. The days of small things are past. We are in a position in America to do great things in a great way. Whatever the horrors of the past war, it illustrated this fact.

We are entirely at odds with the idea that life can be divided into categories. Anything that really lives is bound to take hold upon something beyond itself. The reason why many people have rebelled against religion has been that the religion was too narrow. It did not take account of and provide a place for the cosmos. A religion, however, that is too small to take in everything is too small to do good to anything. We should resent the idea that religion can be shut up to any particular space or to any particular department of life. Hitherto reformations have been attempted through emphasizing the independence of the individual. Future reformations must come about through the recognition of the unity of all nature. And in this definition " nature " must have the largest inclusiveness. It must not be thought of merely as degraded, or as animal, but as the underlying fact in creation whose laws are felt everywhere. There have been times when certain societies of men have thought to make religion more pure by divesting it of beauty. One may as well say that the sunset does not need color. God has ever been too small in human thought. That is because we are human, and inevitably our limited thoughts are limiting our God. We may make our church windows plain, but the color of the sunset will appear there, and the only beautyless spot is a windowless dungeon.

The things done for the first time, which in themselves were good, and good in their effects, were we to make a catalog of them, would make a record such that all men might become optimists. See this fine bridge. It will build another one, and the two will build two more, and the four will build eight. Note this perfect cottage. Someone will copy it. Some arts, indeed, have been lost but a few have been discovered in the same time. What a variety of flowers exist in our gardens! How long a season the gardens have acquired! To achieve all this took time, and love, and patience. But time, and love, and patience were found, and they will be found for everything worth doing.

[*Text continued on page 276.*]

A SPOON RACK. *Dated* 1745

SQUIRREL BRIDGE

Written for picture on page 269 by MILDRED HOBBS

In Elfland, in Elfland
And through the Glen o' Dream
The light of day is shimmering
And silver waters gleam,
And up and down the sky-way
The leaves are weaving laces;
In and out, in and out
The shuttle-wind chases!

In Elfland, in Elfland
A slender bridge is swung
Across the waters glimmering
Where tinkling bells are rung,
And busy squirrels race there
With beech-nuts in their pouches,
Back and forth, back and forth,
To their winter couches!

In Elfland, in Elfland
And through the Glen o' Dream
The squirrels and the faerie folk
Are playing by the stream!
On furry backs the wood sprites
Are riding slender spaces,
Tree folk and wee folk
Under leafy laces!

SWARTHMORE

A PENNSYLVANIA DELL—KITCHEN CREEK

A SQUIRREL BRIDGE—KITCHEN CREEK

DREAM ARCHES—LANESBORO

A PAUSE BY THE ELMS—PROMPTON

YELLOW SHEAVES—WAYNE COUNTY

AN UNTAMED WOOD—KITCHEN CREEK

A LUZERNE STREAM

WATER WORN—LUZERNE COUNTY

THE YOUNG SUSQUEHANNA, NEAR GREAT BEND

THE YOUNG SUSQUEHANNA

Written for the picture facing this page by MILDRED HOBBS

Where the Susquehanna sleeps
Like a lovely child
Cradled by the mountain-steeps,
Pure and undefiled,

In a robe of azure dressed —
Silk without a seam —
Holding lilies on her breast,
Smiling in her dream,

There the trees along the way
Murmur lullabies
Lest the low winds lower sway
And unclose her eyes.

Mossy is her velvet bed,
Grasses hung with beads
Curve above her sleeping head
With the fringing reeds.

Little sailboats painted gay,
Toys forgot in sleep,
Wait for her to wake and play,
Make them dance and leap.

But the Susquehanna gleams,
Peaceful, undefiled,
With the shadowed, sunlit dreams
Of a lovely child.

BEAUTIFY PENNSYLVANIA

IN the course of our peregrinations some features worth making public as assets of beauty, and other features now unsightly which may be transformed, have suggested themselves.

A little way south of Scranton on the way to the Poconos is the Cascade, on page 140. The spot is near the road. An old mill once existed here. The rapid below this little fall is charming. The fall itself passes through a fine rocky formation. Above, for a long distance, the stream glides swiftly over ledges and turns here and there (page 139). It is daintily draped with foliage. No dwellings exist very near at hand. The tract should be secured by the city of Scranton as a natural asset of beauty of much importance. There are cities in the great valley of the Mississippi that would consider this stream and its rocks a marvel to be obtained at any cost. We, who are favored by a residence in broken country, are too apt to overlook many fine features.

THE CORN

RICH brown earth, tending to red. A gentle dip, a gentle rise, repeated to the foot of the hill. The field ploughed and prepared, mellow, and sweet, and deep. Expectant acres, hungry for seed. Under the deep cornice of the shed, a braid of well filled ears, repeated across the whole front. A farmer's boy, barefoot, pacing steadily across the furrowed loam, and striking his planter at the proper intervals. The drenching rains of early May that wash out that boy's footprints in the seeded earth. The tender green shoots rising in the long rows. The careful hoeing. The fight against weeds and frost and pests and drought. The green blades covering the earth. The sturdy serried ranks of August rustling and waving in conscious beauty and victory. The filling up of

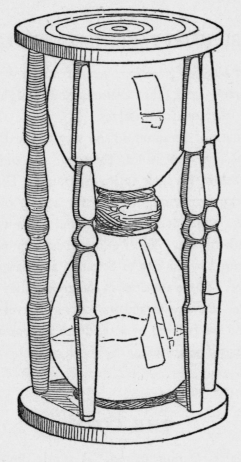

A SAND GLASS

the fine ears, each cased in many garments of green, from the outer cover to the delicate, almost white tissue layer against the kernels. The fine pale clustered strands of silk that hang from the tip of the ear, and depend as gracefully as the locks of the farmer's daughter. The tall spikes, living crosses, held by every stalk in the field. The pollen sifting downward when the whispering breeze hints that the hour has come. The undulations of this living sea in the afternoon, and the dead silence of the fair field under the sunset. The white summer cloud looking down in communion, or the shower which covers all with clustered pearls. The mellowing of the autumn, when the tints change to yellow green, to gold, to russet. The full ear, ten-rowed, twelve-rowed, long, crowded, matt-surfaced with moisture, and colored to the despair of the artist. The cunning blending of sugar in the grain. A cluster of these ears, the acme of wealth and beauty and sentiment. The full harvest, the crown of the year. The glory of the cornfield in spring and summer and autumn, every day changing, every day becoming more perfect, every day telling new tales, stirring new dreams. The grain that greeted our first fathers in America and saved them from destruction; the noblest gift of the Indian to the world.

As the youth and the maiden stand on the margin of the cornfield and pluck the roasting ears, indescribable by any other term than corn color, as they feel the fanning of the summer wind and hear the gentle laughter of the long, broad leaves, as they catch the glint of river, the tips of the forest trees, the gentle rounding of the hill crest, the sweet natural hollow in the field, the fences that the fathers built, and the dear old farm house and barn, they really stand at the centre of life. The corn is the symbol of the best in form, in color, in wealth, in beauty, in faith. What to this is a vineyard, what to this is any other harvest whatever? The corn! A universal food, a perpetual beauty, a joy that renews itself. Pennsylvania may have its mines and its manufactures. It can never get away from the sentiment, the history, the symbolism and the delight of all that is packed so completely, with such deftness, in the green-gowned ear.

THE ORCHARD

PERHAPS a blossoming orchard means as much to the writer as it is likely to mean to anyone. For twenty-five years he has wandered through such orchards, eagerly looking for the stately old trees, the gnarled grace of the limbs, the perfect clusters of a branch. The rows along the field road or the wall, or the isolated trees that decorate the

A FOREST STAIR—LUZERNE COUNTY

WALNUT BANKS—WAYNE COUNTY

A PHILADELPHIA CASCADE

ROBIN HOOD'S BANK

EMBOSOMED—WAYNE COUNTY

A VEILED CRAG—LUZERNE COUNTY

NANTICOKE

sheds, the gables, or the gardens, have been the study of two decades. In a thousand forms, from four o'clock in the morning until eight at night, he has pictured and circled these assemblages of bursting life in its most beautiful form, its finest prophecy. In every quarter of America, as well as on the downs of England and by the roadsides of Brittany, and the flowering cones of the Pyrenees, he has loved and followed and lived with the blossoms. The orchard is nature's sudden spring announcement that we live in a wonder world, a world as beautiful as anything can be, and promising something as luscious as the taste knows, — the health, the sentiment, the poetry and the hominess of the apple tree.

He has here, however, a confession to make, which may shock. As exquisite as is the blossom, he feels that the thickly clustered, parti-colored, crowding, ripe, delicious great apples of October are a finer vision and a dearer mental stimulus than the spring affords. To stand on low steps, one's body surrounded by this draping roof, and to gather the specimens one by one, so perfectly fitting the hand and so appealing in their waxy surface and in their rich coloring, into the cresting basket, until the apex of the arch is filled by one perfect specimen on which a single leaf, which could not bear to part with the fruit, is draped lovingly. This is autumn in her superlative mood. The long rays of a low sun, streaming through the invigorating air of October, and covering the entire hillside with a beauty blended from gold and crimson and green, this is a vision which sums up the year and rounds the fullness of her epic.

When, as often occurs, the apples are seen lying in richly colored heaps to await the curative airs and enriching sun, before being stored, teeming with a distillate of all the secrets and the beauties of the closing year, we have an autumn picture that is indeed superior to the blossoms of May. It is a lamentable fact that it is necessary to arrange this fruit in a certain form, and precision of size, and to place it directly under the eye of the city dweller before she will look at it, still less buy it. Why is it that we cannot believe in our own state, the witchery of our own sunshine, the alchemy of our own airs, the products of our own orchards?

We need a crusade devoted, not to some distant land, but to the unveiling of a Holy Land at home. Is there any reason why distant acres should be more beautiful than yours? Have not your fields, if they are ploughed in hope, and tended in prayer, and reaped in diligence, been made sacred by the use to which you may devote them? Are not these acres where the babies play and the youngsters run, richer in their significance and their moral possibilities, than any distant land?

Why is not your brook, coming from a clean spring which your father faithfully cleared of rubbish and guarded by a stone parapet, why is not your brook, turning about the buttonwood bole, skirting the corner of the garden, as sacred as the streams of the Orient — as stimulating to every fine sentiment as the streams of Greece and Italy?

Life becomes enriched by a keener and a deeper vision. It has in it an ample quota of all those noble elements necessary to adorn the thought of men, to mellow their souls, to form a physical setting of dignity and beauty.

Every morning we need to think over again the story of the Holy Grail to get at the everyday fact that our dear old mother, at the well under the buttonwood, has found our quest. Men are chasing in finance and geography, and in the imagination, to the ends of the earth, and are reaching to other worlds when they merely need to invite the thoughts which are felt in the bosom as a comfortable fire. As we look out over the valley and see its useful stream, its dividing fences, its various crops, and the places of their storage, we are seeing better things than appeared before the eye of Virgil or of any of those who went before him. We have learned that no journey for a Golden Fleece is required. We have arrived at the last, best gift which the natural world has to offer, and that the spiritual world can offer at this period of human development. The main thing is to feel at home here, to work out our relations to the things which are around us, to give approved forms to the things that we touch, to impart grace and strength and to get to be in ourselves the reflexes of our own loves.

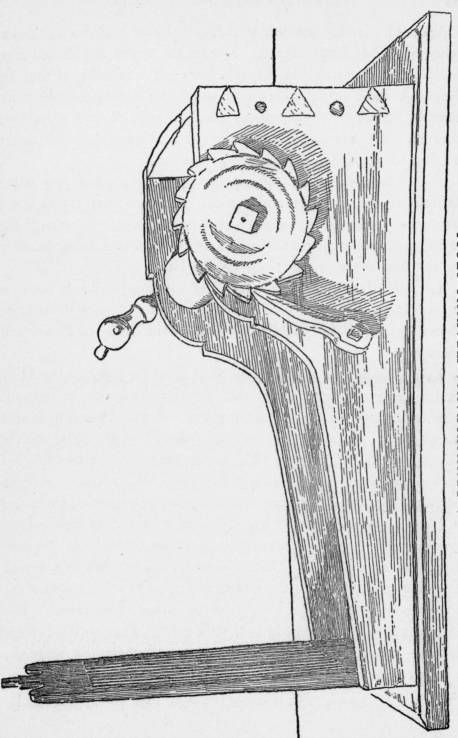

A PENNSYLVANIA WEAVING STOOL

Why is not a maiden in a Pennsylvania valley, gathering the day lilies and the hydrangeas about her own door, and setting her house in order, why is she not potentially the last word in womanhood? If her touch is patient and her thoughts true to the fine things of life, why should anybody ride fast and far after distant graces or charms but little inferior to those on the old stone step under the pear tree? We should, it is true, like to see in Pennsylvania evidences of a somewhat daintier touch, and a translation of life into terms not so closely connected with the purse. The foundations are here. Let there be a shade more of that fine mood which enfolds all things with an ethereal grace, and translates all common life into uncommon delights.

RAMBLING IMPRESSIONS

WE have delighted in threading most of the roads from Bethlehem and Allentown southerly and southwesterly, where so many quaint old villages and farmsteads appear. This is, perhaps, the most interesting district in Pennsylvania to set forth old customs and a gentle rural charm. When the day is dull we confess to having had an eye out for the sign, "Antiques." We have found this district particularly rich in trammels and other fireplace furniture. Near Quakertown, having on that occasion a runabout with a very long, deep back compartment, we were able to fill it almost dangerously full with twisted link or saw-tooth or scrolled trammels, whose owners seemed glad to be rid of them at any figure. This wealth of early iron was found more or less in various neighborhoods as far as Reading, and including that point. On our last journey our inquiries, however, were met by a shake of the head. We were informed that somebody who wrote books about iron and was writing a book about Pennsylvania had been around and gathered up so much that little that was good could be had! We blandly nodded and went on. It was good to be accused of having had a prevision, for once. We were highly amused

A PENNSYLVANIA CHEST.   *J. H. Halford, Owner*

some months later by finding that a committee of two Pennsylvanians was wandering about New England to learn how such Pennsylvania products were valued. If we have taken out of the side of Pennsylvania, when she was asleep, some beautiful creations, we are bound to say that Pennsylvania is no longer asleep. We have even known of Pennsylvanians making pilgrimages to Boston and there purchasing cupboards which came from their own state. It is good that Pennsylvania now cherishes her own, though so many of her own have wandered far before she learned to clasp her children to her bosom. We love the Pennsylvanians for what they have done for us, or for what they have allowed us to do to them!

THE STATELY HOMES OF PENNSYLVANIA

THE Stately Homes of England were treated in a work of that name in a rather stately manner. It may be pertinent to treat the stately homes of Pennsylvania. We refer not so much to those well known historic houses, like the Chew Mansion, as to those splendid great dwellings which have risen in the last forty years in and around Philadelphia, such as the Wanamaker place and a sufficient number of others to fill a great volume. The objection to any immediate enterprise of this sort is partly the lack of mellowness which is a necessary predicate of these homes. Further, they have not exhibited so great a variety in planning and in style as we might suppose the versatility of the American people would demand. Their style is for the most part good. The bad architecture of Pennsylvania consists for the most part in the homes of more moderate size, which have attempted to cover themselves with the merits of all styles, and which therefore have the merit of none. To our thought, the finest type of a permanent home is that which follows the Tudor or Elizabethan motive. It is at once solid, dignified and amply lighted. Its window decoration is very satisfactory, and its roof lines give a fine impression, even from a distance. The abundant materials for such dwellings should foster their

A GRAVE IN THE CLOISTER CEMETERY, EPHRATA

erection, and we have no doubt the coming decade will see a great number erected. In this process, such is the present alertness of architects, and so rich is the region of Philadelphia in architects of fine taste and large experience, that we are not in doubt as to the outcome of the present era of building. We shall have many examples in which the last detail will be worked out with fidelity to the best principles. There is no joy to which we look forward with more avid imagination than to the privilege of examining such homes as they rise.

PENN AND PENNSYLVANIA

THE name of Pennsylvania is poetic and attractive. The state began with idealism and with a touch of poetry. There was, ostensibly and, to a great degree, in reality, a worthy ideal to be fostered as well as a living to be obtained. We like to think that Penn was willing to adventure in the New World without the certainty of a return. It is idle to say that as his grant was far more valuable than its cost to him, even after he had dealt with the Indians, that therefore it was a huge financial deal. There were other ways in which Penn could have used his property in England. With his court entrée the rates of interest were not small, and opportunities for investment were good. Penn really came to the New World largely, at least, for religious reasons. It is something, therefore, that the state was based upon a motive sometimes absent from new enterprises. The outcome proved that Penn in his life-time paid heavily for his idealism. His sons, who were altogether smaller, narrower men, reaped where he sowed.

For all purposes now, thinking of Pennsylvania as a state of mind as well as a geographical location, we want to connect, as far as there is any connection, the idea of the beautiful land that Penn loved, with the present. It was probably not a time when landscapes were as much thought of as they are today. In fact, even when Benjamin West made the famous picture of the treaty under the elm, Penn, being a trifle stout, is as large as the tree, and West has been deservedly criticized that he has not shown a magnificent elm, as he had every opportunity of doing. Thus scenery was not in the eye of the founder or his immigrants, the first, or even the secondary item in their thoughts. But incidentally, good land, like a good horse, is beautiful. The wealth of the trees and the streams, the almost tropic tangle of the vines must have made the state marvellously beautiful. Even today the picture on page 267 suggests the tropics. The marvellously attractive exuberance and variety and majesty of the ancient wood,

SWARTHMORE IN FULL DRESS

THE BORDER OF PHILADELPHIA

A LEBANON BANK

SUSQUEHANNA

A SUBURBAN HOME DRIVE

A PERFECT DAY—WAYNE COUNTY

such as Penn found, bore in upon him the fact that he was the proprietor of country rich in beauty, as in all other particulars. But it is the idealism of Penn, leaping over the sordid money-getting of his sons, that is worth while recalling and applying in Pennsylvania today. The Society of the Friends has suffered much contumely through the centuries. Even the biographer of Penn, or one of them, goes out of his way to hit rather bitterly at sincere men as, when he says, for instance, that money seems to gravitate to martyrs. A bon mot without the shadow of an excuse, beyond the irresistible desire to say a bright thing. We wonder what class of men of whatsoever religious denomination, or of no denomination at all, does not offer a fair butt to ridicule? Dignity itself is always mimicked behind its back by the small boy. The great central fact remains that George Fox enunciated several beautiful and eternal ideas, possibly carried to an extreme, but no less good. Penn thought of Pennsylvania as a vale of peace; no doubt he prayed that it might be so. Nor was he alone in this. It proved necessary, at last, to defend the vale. But the thought of a state made beautiful by serene living, a kind of garden for a friend of God, where God might meet him in the cool of the day, is a thought that we trust may not die. Consciously or otherwise, in the minds of all men, good or bad, there are working suggestions caught through the idealism of other ages. Penn roamed these forests, learned the Indian tongue, and has left us the finest description of Indian life, according to Buell, that appeared from an Englishman in the full century during which it was written. He found the Indian before he had been corrupted by the white man, and he described and admired many fine features of the Indian character. He loved the forests for their own sake and he had in him the strong English delight in park lands. What we hope, and what we think we have reason to hope is that there is a sufficient vitality in certain ideas of Penn to survive the generations, and to blossom forth in a material way in the Pennsylvania landscape. That is to say, we are carrying out in our parking, and in our highways, and in our delightful homes just what Penn himself would have liked to do.

A QUAKER LOVE SONG

By Mildred Hobbs

For thee and me the forests sing,
And for thy feet the meads are flecked
With dainty flowerage of Spring,
And trees are decked!

And when I see thee strolling down
A blossom-bowered road in May,
Soft petals falling to thy gown
Of Quaker gray,

Trimming thy spotless snowy cap
With color bright to match thy cheek,
I would with all the birds, mayhap,
Thy beauty speak.

For if the Lord adorn His trees
And verdant fields with flowers gay,
Shouldst thou His mood the better please
In sombre gray?

The forest sings for thee and me!
And orchard canopies have tried
To make a petal robe for thee,
My Quaker bride!

INDEX